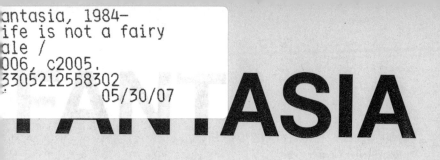

FANTASIA

LIFE IS
NOT
A FAIRY
TALE

A FIRESIDE BOOK
Published by Simon & Schuster
New York London Toronto Sydney

FIRESIDE
Rockefeller Center
1230 Avenue of the Americas
New York, NY 10020

This Fireside Edition 2006

FIRESIDE and colophon are registered trademarks
of Simon & Schuster, Inc.

For information regarding special discounts for bulk purchases,
please contact Simon & Schuster Special Sales at
1-800-456-6798 or business@simonandschuster.com.

Designed by Ruth Lee-Mui

Manufactured in the United States of America

10   9   8   7

Library of Congress Cataloging-in-Publication Data
Fantasia.
   Life is not a fairy tale / Fantasia.
      p.   cm.
   1. Fantasia.   2. Singers—United States—Biography.   I. Title.
ML420.F235A3   2005
782.421643'092—dc22
2005052081

ISBN-13: 978-0-7432-8156-0
ISBN-10:   0-7432-8156-X
ISBN-13: 978-0-7432-8265-9 (Pbk)
ISBN-10:   0-7432-8265-5 (Pbk)

*This book is dedicated to the
most important person in my life, Zion.
Everything I do, I do for you, baby.*

CONTENTS

INTRODUCTION

One night during the *American Idol* competition, Simon Cowell commented on the dance that I had been doing after every song I sang. Walking toward the edge of the stage to hear what the judges had to say was always my least favorite part of the competition. After every song, no matter how good I thought it sounded, my heart would sink, knots would fill my stomach, and my head would suddenly ache with worry about what I was going to hear from the judges. I worried most about Simon. This time, instead of talking about my clothes or my hair or telling me I sounded like Donald Duck, Simon asked, "Fantasia, what is that dance that you do all the time?" Trying to think on my feet, I said, "That's the BoBo!" I made up that word on the spot. I don't even know where it came from or what pushed it out of my mouth. What I should have said was, "That's me gettin' my praise on."

The BoBo is my victory dance. I get my praise on for everything and for nothin' at all. I thank God for my health, strength, and my daughter's working body parts. My BoBo is my way of givin' praise for all of the blessings I receive. When I'm doing my BoBo, I'm aware of all of those who can't do the little things that I'm blessed enough to do.

Everything changed for me during the *American Idol* competition. Just weeks before, me gettin' my praise on was just a personal thing that me and my family did all the time to thank God for what He had done for us and what He would do in the future. Suddenly, even the smallest things about me and my family mattered to the whole world. Everything that was once personal to me and my family was now public . . . like having to explain the BoBo. Everything was different for me. I didn't even recognize myself sometimes. I suddenly had some money in my pocket. I was on TV every week. I had a busy schedule and so many people involved with my daily activities. It was like having ten babysitters. I was meeting all kinds of professionals that I didn't even know had a profession. I had heard of makeup artists, but I never dreamed of someone actually being paid to put makeup on me. I had heard of professional dancers, but I had never met a choreographer. I always thought those people were just dance teachers.

I had spent months on this roller-coaster ride of acting like I knew where I was or what I was doing, but the only moments when I really felt like myself were the moments when I was singin'.

During the competition, I was loving the attention and all the fans who really seemed to love me. They wanted to hug me when they saw me on the street, and sometimes they would run after the car I got in after one of my producers would let me know it was time to stop huggin' folks. I thought those days were crazy. But on the big day, May 26, 2004, when Ryan Seacrest announced my name as the winner of the 2004 *American Idol*, my life changed forever.

Suddenly, I had little boys in wheelchairs wanting my autograph and to take a picture with *me*. I had little girls running up to me in airports and saying, "Look Fantasia, *I* can do the BoBo!" The world had made a dance out of my worshippin' God. I was amazed. And I was a little scared.

I would drive up to shows in different cities—places that I had never been before—and there would be *American Idol* signs all over the place. Small children would be crying from their excitement, and their mothers had to calm them down by stroking their heads. I noticed little girls had gotten their hair cut to look just like mine. Mothers were running with their babies just to get close to the car I was in. I would shrink in fear of what they would do when they saw me. I wasn't worried they would hurt me, I was worried they would be disappointed when they saw me in person. What if I didn't look like I did on TV? What if my lips were even bigger than they thought? What if they thought I was too ugly to be the American Idol? What if they had made a mistake by voting for me? What if my mascara was runnin' because I was cryin' so much? Those were the things that would be flashin' in my head as the limousine pulled up to the stage entrance.

The other thing that would flash through my head was how could I possibly thank them all? Sometimes it was ten thousand people waiting to see *me*. They were wanting to touch me, wanting me to see *them*, wanting me to say something to them that they would never forget. My palms would sweat and my mouth would be dry from the pressure and the excitement of knowing that this was really happening to me. I just kept cryin', prayin', huggin', smilin', and askin' the Lord to get me through those moments like a professional singer, not the messy country girl who had never been too far out of North Carolina.

I thought that being a singer would be enough. Singin' is all I could do, up to that point. I had never learned to deal with so many different types of people. I had never had to see, touch, and smell so many different cultures and vibes. I had never had to love so many people, and I actually *did*. I loved them all for loving me and wanting to see me and touch me, but it was overwhelming at times and I wanted to run and hide. Especially on those days that it rained or it was too hot to wear the outfit that had been chosen for me. Or the times I didn't feel good. Or the days after the nights that I hadn't slept because Zion had been crying on the phone to me. Or the days that I was just feeling guilty for being there inside of this limousine with ten thousand people needing me, while Zion needed me the most.

The excitement of winning has been overwhelming. I have not been used to this much attention in my life except for compliments about my voice and a lot of negative talk about the mistakes in my life. Getting the key to High Point from the mayor left me speechless. I think, How did 'Tasia become the "favorite daughter," when once I was the bad girl to everyone in town?

My shock about all of this comes from the fact that I'm just like these people who come out to see me, who wait in the mall for me, who send me portraits of me that they drew. Just like them, I'm excited by somebody who accomplished somethin', hopin' that their good luck could somehow rub off on me . . . but now that "somebody" is me and *I am trippin'*.

Truth be told, I'm just a young Christian woman with a complicated story to tell. It probably doesn't seem complicated for the girls, like me, who take our laughter and tears in equal doses and feel every day that all the stuff that we go through is just the way life goes. My life only seems complicated for the people who have never been where I started. People who have never even *visited* a poor community where dreams are simply something you do when you sleep.

Most people would never believe some of the things that I've been through, but I'm going to tell you about how I started doing adult things way before I even knew what I was doing. I'm also going to tell you the consequences of those things. I have suffered consequences that I hope even adults will never have to suffer.

I got the idea to write this book because my life has changed in a way that makes me feel like I'm going to bust with nervousness, excitement, confusion, and fear all at once. I couldn't hold all those feelings in anymore. I have been through some crazy things, and I'm finally comfortable enough to talk about them. I can even sit back and laugh at some of them. I still cry about many of them, though. I hope that what I have been through may help people of all ages and nationalities. I hope that this book shows that it is possible to change, no matter what you have done or what has been done to you.

Lastly, I feel like I can say, Chase your dreams, no matter what people say, no matter what *seems* like it is in your way.

Life isn't a fairy tale. It's a real life story—*yours*. Only you can make your own happy ending. Dreams are not just for sleeping.

1. Recognize
Your
Gift

The Bible and my mother always say, "To whom much is given, much is required." That is how I live my life—now. But it wasn't always that way. For most of my young life, much was *not* given. Maybe this saying means that much *hardship* has to be given before receiving the blessings that God intends. *A lot* has been required. But my experiences have shown me that the amount of pain you endure will eventually result in abundance, as long as you stay faithful.

Faith is a legacy for many women in my family, as are the legacies of teen pregnancy, being single mothers, emotional and physical abuse, and poverty. We have all survived it because of the church and our powerful belief in God and prayer. All of the women in my family have had too many experiences for their years, and we seem much older than we are. Most people are surprised that I'm only twenty-one years old. But what seems mature and experienced is just me trying to survive. I have learned and seen a lot in my twenty-one years, but I still have a lot to learn. You will see that as you learn more about Fantasia.

People often ask me: *Who is the real Fantasia?* The answer is: *What you see is what you get.* I would consider myself a very sensitive, outgoing person, and I hope that shows in everything I do and how I treat everyone around me. I care very much about people, probably too much—and I fall in love too easily, as you will see. I am just a country girl who loves the Lord and loves to have a good time. I still kick off my shoes every chance I get—even on TV!

Like all southern folk, I like to have a good time. Country people have had too many bad times, and so we make a good time whenever we can. Although my family lived in High Point, North Carolina, which is technically a small city, we say that this is the country because we have seen big cities like L.A. and New York on TV. Country people place a lot of importance on their families. We rely on our families for every little thing like emotional support, takin' care of our kids, feeding us when we're hungry, or paying our electric bill when we lose our jobs. That's why family is so important to country folks. That's why when you go to the country you will see aunts and uncles living under the same roof with their mothers and other adults. That's why so many grandmothers raise their grandkids when the mothers are too young to handle it. Country folks are really different from city folks because the city folks seem ashamed to tell their families when they are having hard times. For us, hard times are just a way of life. That's the main difference between country folk and city folk that you should know when you read the rest of my story. There is no shame with families like mine. If there was, there would be no families where I come from.

Despite the turmoils and troubles I've had in my life, the things that have always been constants were my mother's support and love. Even when she couldn't be there for me, she kept me lifted in prayer. When I was a teenager and was goin' through so many hardships, my mother was always with me. Really, she *is* me in many ways.

But let me explain by starting at the beginning. My forty-two-year-old mother, Diane Barrino, is a self-proclaimed "country girl" who got pregnant as a teenager. She was nineteen years old. I would say that in some ways, she was luckier than me, and in other ways, I was luckier than her. You'll see as you read my story that much hardship has been required of both of us.

My mother was also raised in the church because her mother, Addie Collins, is a pastor. Just like me, my mother got pregnant by a guy in the church. Of course, she was a singer too and a member of the choir. It was her love of music that brought her together with my father, Joseph. He was in the church quartet and had been asking a lot of questions about my mama. He finally got her phone number, and they started dating. My mother tells us kids that she didn't like my father at first. Mom fell in love with him when she heard him sing. He was able to teach my mother a lot about music because, despite loving it so much, she didn't know anything except how to sing. In her early days, my mother was a *baad* singer. She was raw. She could squall, and her cry sounded like an old woman with many years of grief and wisdom in her spirit.

My mother did have some grief in her past: My grandfather, who was originally from South Carolina, was an alcoholic and abused my grandmother. Grandfather Neil eventually left my grandmother and she was left to raise her three daughters on her own. Grandma Addie's oldest was also named Addie; then there was Diane (my mama), and Surayda. My Grandma Addie had the same dreams for my mother that my mother had for me. Addie's dream was that my mother would go to music school. Right before my mother's pregnancy, Addie had taken her to look at music schools, and they hoped that she would get a scholarship.

Addie had always warned my mother, if you get pregnant you won't be able to follow your dream and become a singer. You won't get to do what the other girls do like go to the movies. And, if you get pregnant, Addie warned, "You will be on your own—no man will help you, and I don't have much to help you with either."

Within twelve months of my parents meeting, my older brother, Kassim VonRico Washington, was born. We call him Rico for short. At the time, my parents were not married, and so his last name is my mother's maiden name. After Rico was born, my mother got a job working in the cafeteria at the Presbyterian Nursing Home while Addie took care of Rico.

Then, eleven months later, my other brother, Joseph, who is named after my father, was born. His nickname is Tiny. That is all we have ever called him.

Family rumor has it that my father's family has Cuban lineage, which would explain my last name—kind of unusual for a black southern man from North Carolina. My father, JoJo, was more gracious than my own "baby daddy." He actually agreed to marry my mother and take care of their two sons. That's why I sometimes say that Mama was luckier than me.

The marriage must have been going well enough because three years later I was born, making the Barrino family five. Grandma Addie was a strong supporter of my parents, sometimes financially, but mostly helping when my mama didn't have enough food for her kids. Most importantly, Addie will go down in history as the woman who crowned me with the crazy name, Fantasia. My grandmother got the name from the Princess House line of fine crystal and gifts. The Fantasia line was supposed to be one of the fancier lines of the gifts. Perhaps my grandmother knew something that I didn't know about how I would turn out.

My parent's marriage was still going strong because nine years later, the Barrino family became six when my mother had my little brother, Xavier. When we kids were small, my mother worked several odd jobs trying to pay the family's seventy-dollar-a-month rent. She worked at hospitals, day-care centers, and sang for anyone in the church who would ask her to sing at their family weddings and funerals.

My father was a truck driver and was away a lot of the time, also tryin' to make ends meet. They struggled along to pay the utility bill, asking for help from whoever had it that month. Even though my father was not at home much, he had a presence in our house. I loved my father because he *stayed*. Most of the kids who lived around us didn't have daddies. The daddies had left, were in jail, or dead. My father seemed to have so much power in anything he did. I will never forget the sound of his boots walking down the hall in the morning. That sound always made me feel secure and that we were better off than the other kids because we had a daddy. I remember secretly watching him from the crack of the bathroom door, which he left open as he shaved. He was always wearing jeans and an undershirt. I thought my daddy was the most handsome man in the world, and I remember watching him worry about every wavy black hair, making sure they were perfect. My father always smelled good, and the strong smell of his aftershave would linger long after he had left the house. His smell just put fear and discipline into my heart and kept me on my best behavior until he came back. All he had to do to discipline me was to *look* at me. When he was coming home from off the road, we just all knew that the king had arrived.

High Point, North Carolina, is about an hour and a half

north of Charlotte. We moved several times to Charlotte and Winston-Salem, neighboring cities that sometimes had better opportunities for my father. We always came back to High Point, though. High Point is actually a very small city with less than 100,000 residents. It is most famous for the furniture outlets where both rich and middle-class people come to buy furniture at wholesale prices. High Point's downtown area is sprinkled with furniture strip malls, and in between the small wood-frame and shingled houses throughout the city, there are churches with names that I will never forget, like Charity Baptist Church, Living Water Baptist Church, Church of Christ, and Galilean Missionary Church. Faith and furniture are the main resources in High Point, North Carolina.

People from High Point are not usually rich. It is a city of workin' folks, and the only money that comes into the city is the money from the bargain hunters looking for furniture. Most people in High Point don't have a lot to be proud of, but they do take pride in being from the furniture capital.

As you drive toward High Point north from Charlotte, the first city is Thomasville, named after the famous furniture manufacturer. The very next city along Interstate 85 is High Point. Although High Point is a major destination throughout the South, it still has a two-lane road as if the city is afraid that one day the people will stop comin'. As you enter High Point, you can feel the pressure of the city as you're trapped in a traffic jam. The first local spot that you see on 85 North heading into High Point is the Paradise

Hotel, which people say is where the drug addicts stay when they've been evicted. My friends used to call High Point the "Land of the Dead," because it was so hard for people to get their voices heard, musically or otherwise. Now, as you cross the city line, there is a billboard of my face that says "Saluting High Point's American Idol, Fantasia Barrino." I still have a hard time looking at it because I can't believe it's there. There is a lot of musical talent in High Point, but no one ever seems to get out far enough to show it to the world or to get a billboard. Most of the people that I knew there ended up strung out on drugs, became drunks, went to jail, had too many kids, or died.

Now, when I drive through the streets of High Point, I'm always happy to see the same old men sitting on the side of Washington Street, drinkin' and tryin' to have a good time. They make me remember that just a few years ago that was Rico, Tiny, and me playing outside with no shoes on. I remember when some of those drunk men used to stumble by when they had their bottle of gin already and an extra dollar and would say, "Come on over here and sing me a song, and I will give you a dollar." I used to stop whatever I was doing, sing the men a song, and get a dollar to buy candy at the Candy Lady who was parked on the corner. Since I was five, singing has always been my life and my livelihood. *Ain't nothin' changed.*

People are poor in High Point because there are not a lot of jobs. If you don't work in a furniture showroom, a hospital, a school, a nursing home, High Point University, a restaurant, or a gas station, there isn't really much more to do. Like I said, my mother worked many jobs to support us. My mother struggled along with Grandma basically raising Rico while she worked and my father was out on the road. After Tiny was born, my father started making more of an effort to take care of his family. My father still wanted to be involved with singing and so did my mother, despite having two little boys. My parents would sing at any opportunity that came to them.

The grandchildren called my father's father "PaPa." PaPa was a singer, too. He was around during the time of the Chitlin' Circuit. The Chitlin' Circuit was a tour route that was only for black artists and it was only in the South. It was the only place that a black singer could get a gig. It was hard on the Chitlin' Circuit, because although it was designed for black singers, it was still the South and sometimes bad things happened to the musicians that were travelin' in the South. PaPa never got over that. He has a lot of anger and no trust for the music industry, so he wouldn't let his sons leave and try to earn a living as musicians. The older brothers rebelled and went anyway, but my father, the youngest, was not allowed to go. The Barrino Brothers consisted of my uncle Perry, uncle Jute, and uncle Nate. They traveled all around the Carolinas singin' and makin' music. All of my grandfather's boys, including my young father, were so in love with music. I don't think my father ever got over not being able to sing with his brothers and his anger over that motivated him to make his own band and put me where I am today.

My earliest memory of music was when I was about five years old. My parents used to sing at weddings and they would take us along. Their big wedding song was Natalie Cole's "Inseparable." They used to sing it and it sounded so good to me. All kinds of feelings would wash over me when I heard them singin' that song. I would watch them and I could actually feel the love that song was tryin' to express. It made me think that being married was a great thing.

Rico and I would imitate them in the bathroom at home. We would imitate all the facial expressions and hand gestures. We would stand up on the toilet and make sure our facial expressions made us look like our parents. My brother used to practice putting his hand underneath my chin, just like my father used to do to my mother.

One day, my parents heard us imitating them and came to see our bathroom show. They were impressed, and the next time they sang at a wedding, my father introduced Rico and me as the "couple" who was going to perform "Insepara-ble." We were shocked that my father did that, but we had practiced it so much in the bathroom, we just knew we could do it. I remember walking to the microphone. I was nervous at first. Remember, I was just five. I looked over at Rico, and he smiled at me and made me feel better. The first note that I hit made the bathroom scene come to life for me and I was no longer nervous. The further along in the song we got, the more I could feel the audience's reaction.

People were amazed at how good we sounded. My fa-ther got so many compliments that he decided to put the family together and form a group. We were called the Barrino Family. We toured the Carolinas and other cities in the South, blessing church services, revivals, and concert halls with our sweet harmonies and moving lyrics. The Barrino Family was famous for the little five-year-old girl with a grown woman's voice. That was me— 'Tasia. People used to tell my parents they couldn't believe that such a big voice was comin' out of such a little girl! I sometimes think all of my mother's dreams for her musical career were rolled up into my big voice. A voice that was given to me by God.

In the band, my dad played bass and directed us kids, and my mom wrote the songs and gave us the key to sing in. I was the one who wanted to sing all the time. I never complained. I was too young to understand all of the details of being on the road and needing money to sustain us. All I knew was that I was a singer and that meant everything to me—even when I was five. Singing was the only place I ever wanted to be. Rico also loved singing, but Tiny had another idea about being on stage. Tiny always wanted to be "cool," and he felt that he couldn't go to school and be cool the next day with a reputation of being in his family's gospel group.

My father was a perfectionist and struggled with creating a band with three kids as the key members. His perfectionism was hard for us to deal with, and he was equally frustrated by our childish imperfection. We would practice the songs every day until they were just right. He would make us stay up until one and two in the morning, until the song was just how he wanted it to be. He was equally hard on all of us if we weren't perfectly clean and neat or if one hair was out of place. And when he came home, if the house wasn't spotless, I would get into big trouble. My father needed everything to be perfect: the music, the house, and his appearance. It used to take my father three hours to get dressed. I remember him being so clean-cut and well dressed. I still love to see a well-dressed man. All of my father's unfulfilled childhood dreams seemed to have been haunting him and making him mean. When we would perform, Rico and I did everything we could to do our best—if for no other reason than just so we didn't disappoint Daddy. I always remember that look on his face when he was happy. His face shined with pride and ownership.

Whenever we would have a bad performance, I remember my father fussin'. He would say angrily, "You need to do better. Remember your notes!" Tiny was always in trouble. But Tiny never cared about my father's reaction, so he would come to the stage with a hairbrush and start brushing his hair on stage in the middle of a song. Rico and I were always too scared to do anything like that. I will never forget when Tiny took that brush out and started brushin' one time and my father went to the stage and smacked him on his head. Only once do I remember him being mad at something that I did. I poked my lips out and acted mad in front of other people. My father popped me. I was so upset because I never did anything wrong. I was so ashamed of getting a beating in public. It never happened again.

We continued performing and were becoming known as

the family that could sing. We traveled whenever we could, just for the exposure. We went to Alabama, Mississippi, throughout the Carolinas. We appeared in churches, in revivals, at fairgrounds, and anywhere else that wanted us. Sometimes we didn't have enough money to pay for food and we would eat Vienna sausages and chips and call it a night. Sometimes, if we were lucky, we would sleep at someone's house from the church that we were visiting. Other times we would just sleep in the van. I never complained because I was doin' what I wanted to do—sing. I can still see myself in the mirror with my pretty church dresses, white stockings, and Shirley Temple curls all over my head.

As I started to grow up, I realized that I had a gift. I began to understand that the purpose of our music was no longer to satisfy my father, but to glorify God. Every time I took the microphone, my intention was to give my gift back to God. My singing started savin' souls and changin' lives. By the time we left a church, people would be shoutin' in the aisles, givin' praise to God, singin' and prayin'. I noticed even young people were being moved by my gift.

We were blessed early on. A record company based in the South approached us. But my father had been too quick to sign the contract. His childhood dreams were causing him to act without thinking. The rest of us didn't know enough or were too young to question his decisions, although they sounded a little fishy to my mother, who had warned him not to sign anything. My father signed anyway. We finally started seeing a little bit more money, but when the CDs came out, there was no mention of my mother as songwriter for any of the songs, and she had written them all. Someone else's name was listed as the songwriter and, because my father had signed the papers, there was nothing that we could do except watch our money go to someone else. My mother was too hurt even to speak about it since she had told him not to sign the deal. We had been taken. We were running out of money, quickly, and at the same time, our records were playing on the radio every day and our albums were selling out throughout the Carolinas. We were getting bookings, but we had no band because we had gained a reputation for not payin'. No one would work for free.

The last band that we had disappeared. They missed several rehearsals. Finally, they came over one night to apologize for their recent absences and to break the news that they had signed with Universal Records and were going on the road with a signed artist. It was a depressing time for the Barrino Family.

We had no money, but we were blessed with my mother's brother, Uncle Sonny, who always helped us when we most needed it. Uncle Sonny could always be relied on to get us some tuna sandwiches and French fries or some fried bologna or some money to pay a bill.

My brother Tiny finally got the nerve up when he was thirteen years old to tell my father that he didn't want to sing with the family anymore. He left the group to start working on his own musical interest in R&B. Rico left the group when he was fifteen for the same reason. He formed a group called Infinity Three. I didn't leave; I wasn't going anywhere.

We got more singers, and we recorded an album. I was twelve years old then. The album was called *Miracles*, and that's what it was.

Soon after, we kids really started pullin' away from the family. The boys had already left the band, and I was starting to be out with my friends. My mother, upset by the bad deal that my father made, was fallin' deeper and deeper into depression. My father was not supporting her—or us—at all. As hard as times were in that house, I still have good memories of that time because music lived in 511 Montlieu Avenue with us. It was the place where everyone in the neighborhood would gather to sing. Family members and neighbors would come over and sing. People who *couldn't* sing would come over to our house to sing. Our house was the popular house and although we struggled—sometimes eatin' grits every night for a week—we had good times. We all grew up listening to different types of music. Old music was the music with the joy in it. As children, my parents had us listening to Aretha Franklin, Anita Baker, Luther Vandross, Stevie Wonder, Ella Fitzgerald, and Christian groups like Paul Porter and the Christianaires. We were learning to recognize scatting and riffs and squalling. We could all point out a good riff. We knew how to harmonize and sing bass, alto, or tenor. All of my father's siblings were singers, and music was the legacy that he gave us.

My family sang because it was replacing all the things

that we wanted and needed and didn't have. Music was our bread and water. Our next-door neighbor was an older woman, and she used to come over and say, "Y'all are making so much noise, but I am not going to call the police, because your singin' is blessin' my soul."

To this day, my mother says how amazed she is at my talent and how God's spirit fills me. The only way she describes how music first came into my life is: "When 'Tasia started singing, she was always singin' and cryin', singin' and cryin'."

That has not changed a bit.

Our first church started in my grandmother's basement. My mother told me that Grandma Addie was beaten to a pulp by her drunken husband. She had three daughters who also had children too young, and she was worried about her own soul and the soul of her family. She decided that she had to do something. Grandma Addie prayed and asked the Lord to set her family straight. As Grandma tells it, the Lord told her to open the door of her house to let the Holy Spirit in. God spoke to my grandmother in a vision of a church in the basement of her house.

My grandmother lived in a small, red-brick house with sagging wood floors. The basement had a separate entrance from the back of the house, and the congregation would use that door to enter the church. My family would enter through the door in the hallway that led down to the basement. We had about eleven members initially, and my family made it eighteen in total.

What finally became the church had been the carport before my grandmother had the vision. One day she met a man at the produce market and she was telling him about her vision for the church and the young man happened to be a contractor. He told my grandmother, "I think I can help you do that, Miss Addie." A couple of days later he came to the house, measured it out, and he created a room that would eventually host the Holy Ghost. Because it was the carport, the heating and plumbing were all exposed, and my grandmother couldn't afford to change the ceiling, so she just left it. She was blessed to be able to install heating and cooling eventually. But back then, the humid North Carolina summers were hotter than hell in that church. The exposed insulation on the ceiling meant the congregation had to duck down to sit in certain seats.

My grandmother had bought a wooden cross that she draped with purple velvet, which she had seen in the initial vision of the church. The cross was placed in front of the furnace. As my grandmother says, "We're havin' chu'ch in there!"

The phrase "havin' chu'ch" reminds me of when the Bible says that when two or three are gathered, God is in the midst. All of us believe that strongly. When we have our "chu'ch," we're just praising God with our love and our actions toward each other. And we are always prayin' about something and singing. Prayer is just our norm as a family.

Back then, when the eleven members started telling their friends about the Holy Spirit who made it to my grandma's house every Sunday, we had to move into a store-front because the home church wouldn't hold that many people. Less than a year after the storefront, we had grown to about 100 or 150 members. Then even more people started comin' and wantin' to be a part of Mercy Outreach, which is what my Grandma Addie named her church. The word on the streets of High Point was that Mercy Outreach was the church of the Barrino Family. Everyone wanted to be blessed by our voices. Finally, we were able to move the church again, this time into a real church building with a sign out front with my grandmother's name as pastor and my mother's name as the associate pastor. The church has cush-ioned pews instead of the white folding chairs and a pulpit that would make any preacher proud. The church grew to be about 250 members.

The church is my grandmother's heart. Because there was a lot of drama, as there sometimes is in the black church, we started losin' members after about a year. People started leaving because of all the talk of sinnin' that was goin' on. There was talk about my father and how he was dating some of the women in the church. Baptists don't like to be in-volved with a sinnin' church. They think just being near sin will mess up their chance of gettin' into Heaven. There was a lot of talk and gossip about the church and around the church, while Sunday services kept gettin' smaller and smaller. The contents of the tithing basket were also getting smaller. Suddenly the mortgage payments were getting fur-ther and further apart. My grandma was stressin' because she thought she would be failing God if she lost the church. She continued to pray and put Mercy Outreach back into God's hands, where it belonged.

As I got older, I used to pray to God that if He would raise me out of my situation, I would bless my grandmother with the money she needed to save Mercy Outreach. God answered my prayer by blessing me with *American Idol*, and my grandma's church still stands today.

Being in church was—and still is—my most peaceful place. When I'm there, I go over a lot of things in my mind. If I have any worries or stress, I let them all go the moment that I walk into the church. Church is also the place where music came to life for me. It was the place I could have a good time, hear good music, and clap my hands.

All this shoutin', witnessin', and praisin' all looked normal to me as a child. My family talks about how my mother was shoutin', prayin', and singin' when she had me in the womb. People used to say she was going to shout that baby right out! Even though I could be a part of everyone singin' and praisin' God, I still had to experience it *within*. One Sunday, when I was around five or six, I was up singin' and something just hit my body. It was like a violent strike to my soul. I didn't know what it was. I couldn't explain it. The feeling took me to my knees. I don't know what I looked like kneeling up there with that feeling rushing through me like warm water. I will never forget it. I asked my mother what had happened, and I remembered her saying, "You have the Holy Ghost. You now have a relationship with God." She was right. That was my very first love affair. I was anointed. That anointing made me see that music was my gift. Back then, church and music and God were all connected as one. By recognizing that God was within me when he gave me my voice, I finally knew that I was special.

Praisin' God with song is the main reason for bein' in the Holiness Church in the first place. Holiness is the only way I know how to be. When someone feels the presence of the Holy Spirit, they need to let it out! Sometimes, the spirit makes us run up the aisles of the church; sometimes it makes us sit still and cry; sometimes it makes us faint. I have fainted. But most of the time it just makes me do my dance, the BoBo.

People who have never experienced Holiness often ask me, "What is it like?" I get that question a lot. Holiness is not somethin' that I can easily describe, but because I'm tellin' it all, I'll try my best.

When I walk into the church, I'm always moved by the sense of order in the room. Church is the only place that people seem to act like they have some respect. Everyone is always dressed neatly and modestly. The walls of the sanctuary are starch white, like new Easter clothes. The mahogany pews are always polished in anticipation of the high emotions that will fly around them, wetting them with sweat and tears. The same wooden cross that was part of that first basement church is hangin' right there at the pulpit. It's draped with the same purple velvet that Grandma saw in her vision. The pulpit is small, with six white upholstered chairs arranged in a semicircle where the ministers sit. The choir sings below the pulpit when they are called. The church has an impressive sound system and features a bandstand, which shows that music is a part of my family's ministry and is a part of every aspect of our family's life.

Once I sit down, I carry on—shoutin', praisin', and doing my BoBo. I always carry on that way when I'm in church. It's the only place that I feel free enough to let myself loose. The wood pews are a comfort to me when I fall in exhaustion at the power of the spirit in the church.

During the praise and worship service, people who are feeling somethin' come up and speak about what had happened to them during the last week. They discuss a health problem that has been resolved or a new diagnosis that has scared them and talk about how they are afraid that they're goin' to die. They mention family members who are in trouble, sick, or who have died. Most importantly, they speak about what God had done for their life in the last seven days. They talk about the ways that God has healed and solved a problem and had strengthened them to handle whatever it was.

At that point, I always cry. Everyone in the congregation, including me, listens and agrees with the power of God. Hearing these stories relieves my stress and everyone else's. It makes me feel that I'm not alone in my struggles. It makes me feel the need to say something out loud. Some say, exuberantly, "Yes, God!" or "Praise the Lord!" I say in agreement, "Yes, He did!"

Within several minutes, after the opening songs have been sung and the visitors have been welcomed, the feeling in the air escalates and everyone is thinkin' about how God has helped them or healed them. Everyone in the room is thinkin' of their own miracles that God has performed. My mother used to tell me that she would always think about me and how God had shown me and our whole family favor, despite the mistakes that we have made.

Looking around the sanctuary and seeing women and children cryin' and grown men runnin' up and down the aisles of the church as if they were runnin' for their life— or runnin' from their demons—always moves me. It shows me how fragile we all are. Graying women put down their crutches and jump up and down as though they were exercising. Women sitting next to me begin to shake and quake. I would see them tumbling to the ground. Beads of sweat drench everybody's foreheads. A woman in a white nursing uniform once pushed me aside to comfort a fallen woman, while I yearned for the breeze of the white blanket to be fanned over my wet head, too.

People scream and shout around me. There are clusters of people behind me repeating: "Yes, Lord, yes, Lord, yes, Lord . . ." as though they are under a spell. Another chorus from the front is chanting, "Thank you, Lord. Thank you, Lord. Thank you, Lord." A younger woman two rows ahead of me is repeating "Hallelujah! Hallelujah! Hallelujah!" The musicians in the front of the pulpit are playing a tune that is hyper and jubilant, yet everyone is cryin' and fallin' down. I hear unintelligible phrases coming out of my own mouth— that is me speaking directly to God, but others call it "speaking in tongues."

People are losing their balance all around me. Some are humbled and on their knees. Others are sitting in their seats upright and calm. A young girl is waving her arms like she will fly away. I feel myself going in and out of consciousness. I stand up with new energy and find myself running in place, with my shoulders hunched and my arms in the running position. My fists are balled up as if I'm beginning to box. I have a smile on my face that is blinding. I am doing the BoBo.

The minister, my grandma Addie, comes to the center of the pulpit with the comforting clouds that she had painted above her as an imaginary "Heaven above." She is calm and serene and says these simple words, "The Holy Ghost is in the house! Amen." And she waits until the Spirit takes its time and tames itself.

That is how it is in a Holiness church.

This is the place where the BoBo lives.

Whenever I go to church, I think hard about what God has done for my life and how he continues to appear in my life, like a daily miracle. I think about the dreams and visions where He came to me and told me the things that I needed to hear. I think about how I got into the *Idol* audition when it wasn't even possible. I think about Zion and how she turned my "bad" act into a blessing. I think about my mother and how she has stood by me through everything. I think about how blessed I am to have her. I cry every time I think about my cousins, Kima and Kadijah, who don't have their mother, Aunt Rayda, anymore, because she was murdered. I think about my father and how he built my career by leading all of us kids to music. I think about the small, lopsided three-bedroom house at 511 Montlieu Avenue with all its memories of music, family, friends, and hunger . . . and how far we all have come. I think about all the places I have been to around the world. I think about how amazing it is that my singing got me out of High Point and out into the world. I think about the anointing I have with my voice and how powerful it is for others.

Thinkin' about all these things, I start to feel full. I feel full of pain and joy all at once. I feel regret for those who don't know about God's love. I feel proud that I do know His love firsthand. I think that there is evidence of Him every-where. These thoughts and feelings come up like a wave. It's unexpected and I feel more tears coming. I feel my mouth twisting up to hide the wail inside my soul. These thoughts cause me to shake with excitement and gratitude. I think of my amazement at all the blessings that have come to me, a girl who was undeserving so many times, but God continued to give me chances time and time again. I feel a tightness in my body. I feel like I'm going to burst with joy and gratitude. These feelings cause me to rise out of my seat. I start to shake myself away from earthly concerns and worries. Standing in the church, my mind travels to a private place and I feel like I'm no longer there.

What brings me back to the church is the young people who seem bored and uninterested in church. Many young people who I have met and even some of my old friends seem ashamed to show off their faith in God, which has always been so natural to me that I can't really understand them. They seem embarrassed to flaunt their relationship with God. Most young people would much rather talk about their relationship with a man or a woman. Most people would rather flaunt their new clothes or their new bling-bling. I always wonder why God is not worthy of praise and acknowledgment? Why are young people ashamed to show their faith? Take it from me—faith is really all you have.

Through lots of patience, God has shown me how to use my precious gift of music. It was a difficult journey just to find the gift that God had already placed inside of me. He has done the same for you—he has given you an extraordinary gift. You just have to have faith and he will lead you to it.

MY MOMENT OF
FAITH: WHAT I LEARNED

For unto whomsoever much is given, of him shall be much required.

LUKE 12:48

Make a joyful noise unto the Lord, all ye lands. Serve the Lord with gladness: come before his presence with singing.

PSALMS 100:1–2

- I believe that there is a God, the man who wakes up every morning and puts breath in our bodies. He is the creator and He is an awesome and mighty God. He can do anything. He is an on-time God. He may not come when you want Him, but He will be there.
- I like to go to the ocean and see the miracles that God has created. It reminds me of His power. He can do anything, like pulling me up from where I came, taking me through what I have been through, and bringing me to this point—the point where I prayed to be my whole life.
- I have been praising God since I was five years old. I continue to thank Him and bless Him every day. I could have given up long ago. God has a hand upon my life. God has put me here for a reason. Maybe He has put me here to share what it means to recognize the gifts that God has given you and hold on to them with everything you have. God's gifts are real.

- Music has been in my life and in my mind and in my body from the very beginning. It is and continues to be my most sacred form of expression. By acknowledging that music was my gift, I was able to lean on it and rely on it when there was nothing else.
- Everybody gives God praise in his or her own way. Find your BoBo! In whichever way you want to thank God, you can, but just be sure you do it.

2. You
Made Your Bed,
Now Lie in It

Looking for your gift can be painful. It's a journey that requires that you go through things. I must have been looking for my gift for years. Even though people were constantly praising me about my voice, I wasn't listening. I was searching for my gift but didn't know it was as simple as it being my singing voice. I was like a dog chasing her tail. I knew it was there, but I couldn't hold it in my hands.

So I made some mistakes in order to find my gift and find myself. They were big mistakes because I was sittin' in High Point with nothin' to do, no money, no plans for the future, no role models of people who had left High Point, and only the "borin'" reminder that God and church were always the only thing to do for the rest of my life. Like most twelve and thirteen-year-olds, I was restless, and going to church four days a week was wearin' thin. By now, my brothers had left home and left the singing group and I was lonely in every way.

My heart was empty and seeking somethin' to do. I cried a lot because I could feel God's spirit pulling me toward Him and boredom pulling me toward trouble. *Trouble won.*

It was a feeling too overwhelming to describe. The confusion of curiosity and possible danger mixed with God's pull on me made me weepy and sad. The heat of being frisky and "grown" just took over me and made me feel like cryin' even more. Although I had been anointed when I was five, I didn't realize that my anointing was God's special gift. I took it for granted. As I got more curious about the world, God's grip was loosened and His mysterious ways started to kick in. And little by little I could feel myself beginning to change— and not for the better.

Let me go back a little. When I was a child, I was always so skinny and I had big lips. People teased me about it all the time. I used to go home to my mother and cry and tell her that everyone thought I was ugly. It's lonely when you feel like you're not good enough. When I got a bit older, I started imitating the girls I admired. I wanted to be like the girls who had it "goin' on"—the ones with fingernails, makeup, and cell phones. The girls who got their hair done. I thought that if I was like them, I would be happy. Happiness was my gift, I thought.

So, after years of growing up in the church, I went astray.

I left the church with the idea that I was going to fit in with all the other girls, the girls who were not in church but seemingly having all the fun. I was going to fit into the world.

By the time I reached the eighth grade and was going to T. Wingate Andrews High School, "sex, sex, sex" was all everyone was talking about at the lunchroom table every day. All the girls were talking about how fun it was and how *good* it was. I didn't have anything to say about it because I wasn't "doin' it." I wasn't even thinking about how sex would feel or what it would do for me. I started dating the pastor's son, who I'll call B. He was sixteen years old and I was fourteen. B. tried to convince me to have sex with him. He talked and I listened. All I was thinking was that if I didn't have sex with the preacher's son, he would find someone else who would be willing and he would leave me behind. Finally, he convinced me. I didn't know nothin' about nothin'. At best, I was "tryin' to have sex."

After we had done it, I was disappointed. It wasn't anything like I had hoped. I thought sex would make me see fireworks and make my temperature go up. I thought it would change everything for me. And, I guess it did. Sex didn't feel good at all. It just felt like loneliness. The next day I sat down at lunch and said to my girlfriends, "It was not all you said it was. It isn't *all that*." I think my main disappointment was that B. really didn't care anything about me. But I didn't say that to them. I figured I just needed more practice.

I thought that I was in love. B. had taught me *everything* I knew about sex, even how to French kiss. He was two years older than me and more experienced, so I thought he held the world in his hands. I was head over heels in love with him. I thought he couldn't be bad: he was the preacher's son.

After a while, I started to feel more independent and rebellious, like I didn't want to hear anyone's opinions or thoughts about my life. I didn't want to hear from my mama about what I was wearin'. I didn't want to hear from my daddy about what time to come home. I didn't want to hear from anybody about how I was doin' in school. The only person I wanted to hear from was B. Anything he said was OK. I was *gone* over this guy. I used to follow him around. I was always calling him and going to the mall, where he and his friends were hangin' out. I would show up just so that he could see me and be reminded that I was there. He never went looking for where I was unless we had planned it. And then he would be late or not show up at all. That should have been a sign to me that our love was one-sided.

I was so busy chasing B. around, I was messin' up in school. Going to school became inconvenient for the chase. There were too many rules. I felt like an independent woman in the way I was dressing and in my actions. The people at my school just thought I was a bad kid. The boys at school didn't think of me as a woman—they thought of me as a "ho."

I hated having to be in school and hated having to be at class at a certain time. I hated the teachers and I hated not being able to spend all my time with my boyfriend. I thought that I was grown up and that I didn't need any of this anymore. I felt this even stronger now that I was "in love." I was frisky at the time, too. As the older women from church used to say, "I was smellin' myself," kind of like a female dog in heat. My body was hot all the time. I wanted to wear little clothes and get attention from boys. I remember one skirt that I made where I cut the hem so high up that you could see everything that I should have been keeping sacred.

B. and I continued to see each other every opportunity we had and slowly my thoughts on sex changed from disappointment to *need*. I would sneak out every opportunity I got to be with him. I skipped school regularly so we could be together. The misunderstanding at that time was that I thought we were in love with each other and he thought that I was easy.

The next misunderstanding I had to deal with changed me forever. I was raped. I want to share this with you because if I can save one of you from having to go through this, like I did, this story is worth sharing. Girls, I know so many of you have had the same thing happen to you, which makes me so mad, sad, and worried for my daughter, Zion. But as long as I'm telling it all, I may as well be as open and honest as I can be. I don't want to leave nothin' out.

One day a popular guy in school gave me more attention than I wanted. I was seeing B., but there was always someone new to flirt with and he was one of the guys I always wanted to notice me. It made me feel good to get attention from the guys. When I was wearing something short, I would make a point to go up to this one particular guy and wave, or brush against him by accident, or drop something in front of him. Finally, he noticed me. He raped me in the auditorium after school. I can barely recall the details. I just know that I shudder to think of how that single act changed me in a way that I didn't need to be changed. I remember pulling myself together and going down to the girls' locker room and hiding. I was thinking to myself that I was goin' crazy. I could hear my own voice saying, "It's your own fault. You was friskin' around." I was shaking like a leaf behind a wall of lockers hiding my face and speaking into my tear-drenched hands. I hid in the locker room until everyone had left the gym and the school. When I finally walked the long road up Montlieu Avenue, I went straight to bed. I didn't get out of my bed for two days. When my mother asked me why I wouldn't go to school, I said simply, "I'm not going." I was too paralyzed to even wash the rape off of me. I felt *filthy*.

Finally my mom came to me and said, "Something has happened to you." I didn't even have to tell her, she could see it all over my face. I told her exactly what happened. She took me back to school, marched me into the principal's office, and forced me tell them the name of the boy who raped me. He ended up getting into some trouble, but not the trouble he deserved for stripping me of the little innocence I had left.

I dropped the case with the police, because I was constantly being harassed by the other guys in school who used to taunt me with "I'm going to do the same thing that he did to you." They were friends of the guy who raped me. I was their joke. They were laughing while I was slowly dying inside.

Being raped was just another reminder that I was losin' control of myself. All those short skirts and frisky ways were gaining me nothing, and I was losing any pride that I had left. I was so ashamed that rape happened to me. I was so helpless and powerless. At the time, I wondered if it was partially my fault, because of the message that I was sending out, with my actions and dressing that way and being so . . . frisky. Looking back, now I realize that this was my main misunderstanding in high school: I was trying to be one thing, which I thought was grown up and independent, but other people thought I was something else. I couldn't bring myself to either side of the misunderstanding, mature like I thought I was or the "ho" that I had portrayed for the boys. I was neither one.

Eventually my family moved to Charlotte. We moved because my father had found a small house and was working with a trucking company. My mother was growing depressed and my father wanted our family to make a new start.

In Charlotte, I started going to a new school, and I was making better grades than I ever made in High Point, although my grades were never really great. I thought I was finally separating myself from my past, forgetting the rape and becoming humble again. I wanted to learn and be smart, for once. But being so focused on school was not enough for my spirit. I had no friends at the new school. I desperately wanted to go back to High Point, because I was lonely. I missed my friends and I missed my boyfriend.

After many family debates, I was allowed to move back to High Point and stay with my grandmother. When I got back to High Point, I never went back to school. But I went back to B.'s arms. I had officially dropped out of school in the ninth grade. My mother was depressed and she knew that whatever she said, I wouldn't listen. The fact that I had stopped going to school didn't even come to her attention for a couple of months. My grandmother was too involved with her church, and what I didn't tell her, she didn't know.

My grandmother had given up on me and decided to let me see what life was really about. *My mother had given up on herself.* Things with my parents had gotten rough. None of us were getting along. At my parents' home, there was always fighting. I was arguing with my father, my mother was arguing with my brothers, my mother was arguing with my father. My parents were fighting every day about money and the fact that they didn't ever have enough. My mother was accusing my father of being with other women and he just kept saying that he wasn't cheating on her.

My mother had once been a very vocal person with a lot of spunk. As their relationship got worse, my mother said less and less to my father and everyone else. I moved out of my grandmother's house and was staying with my friend, Tonya, who was living in the projects. Tonya was thirty years old at the time. I wasn't really doing anything with my days, except for watching TV and hangin' out with older women. Tonya didn't work; she was receiving assistance, so we were home together a lot, watching her child. I no longer wanted to listen to my mom, although she wasn't ever really strict with me. She never tried to pressure me. She let me make my own mistakes. But what she really did was let me go.

My mother's mounting depression allowed her to let me go so easily. She was frustrated because she couldn't be a role model herself, so she had nothing to show me or tell me about doing the right thing. She had married too soon, had children too soon, and didn't have an education or a way out of the situation she was in. She had done everything I was doing, so I guess she felt like she couldn't judge me.

At the age of seventeen I started going to clubs. I was drinkin', smokin', and partyin'. I wasn't even old enough to be drinkin', and I was already partyin' like an adult woman. When I should have been getting ready to graduate from high school with other kids my age, I was hanging out with these older women who were supposed to be my friends. These older women friends were buying drinks for me and I was drinkin' them.

I was still seeing B., off and on, and having sex with him. Although I thought I was *so* in love with him, we weren't even a couple.

Pretty soon, my period didn't come. I realized that I was pregnant. I was still living with Tonya. She was already a baby mama with one child of her own. She knew that I was pregnant without me even having to say the words. One day I woke up, ate breakfast, and threw it all up on Tonya's kitchen table. Tonya said, "Girl, what is wrong with you?" I was so embarrassed looking at the mess that I had made on the tabletop. I said, "I threw up," and as soon as I said it, Tonya and I both knew. Tonya came over to me, shook her head, and said, "Girl, you may be pregnant." I knew I was.

I couldn't call my mother because she would have either gone crazy or just said nothing at all, which is how she had been responding to me for the last year. I called my brother, Tiny. He and I were both party animals. He took me to the health department for the free pregnancy test. If you are pregnant, the health department counselor asks you some simple questions: *Do you want to keep the baby? Do you want to have an abortion? Or do you want to have the child and then give it to someone else?*

It wasn't a hard decision. I looked at the light green walls of the clinic and I thought: *I am not getting rid of this baby. This baby was my own doing. I was out there being "grown" and left school, the church, and my family. I made my bed, and I am going to lie in it.* I also couldn't help but think that my mama could have gotten rid of Rico or Tiny or me, and I wouldn't be here today talkin' about it.

I told the counselor that I was going to keep my baby. The counselor sent me off to become yet another baby mama.

I dreaded telling my friends and family because I knew they would be mad at me. Most of them already had babies who were missing daddies. Because of my singing, people would be shocked that I fell into the High Point baby trap. People don't understand that singin' in the church doesn't make you free from curiosity—or sin. Maybe it makes you even more curious—and more likely to experiment with the things that we were taught to avoid.

Tiny and I went to my grandmother's house to break the news to my mother, who was living there at the time. My family members were in constant motion due to the marital problems that my parents were having.

Tiny walked into my grandmother's house in front of me. He went over to my mother, holding the papers from the health center in his hands, and said, "Mama, I took her up there." The high teen-pregnancy rate in High Point made the reference to "taking her up there" obvious. Every mother in High Point knows that "going up there" means that her little girl had a pregnancy test and was bringing home news of a grandchild.

"She's pregnant," Tiny said to my mother. My mother didn't say anything at first. I stood in the background, just cryin' and cryin'. My mother let out a squall that came from the bottom of her soul. My grandmother, Addie, was shaking her head, already knowing for weeks, because I had been coming to her house in the afternoons and sleeping until dark. "I knew that gal was pregnant," Grandma said. "I just knew it." My mother kept squallin' and started saying, "No, not again. Not again!"

I was cryin' because I had disappointed my mother, *again*. I had left the church, I had left school, and now I was going to have a child, just like she had. It was the very way that my mother had lived her life that I was trying to avoid. Suddenly, all those talks about sex and babies and protection and the things that boys would say to get you to "do it" came floodin' back into my mind. We used to sit up late into the night talkin' when I would come home late after hangin' out. My mother would sit up and wait for me, every time.

In that single moment, standing with my grandmother, my mother, and myself, all young mothers, I had stepped into the darkness of what my mother called the "generational curse." That saddened me the most.

The next person to tell was B. I sensed he would be the most upset. I was too worried about what his reaction would be to meet with him in person. I decided just to call him. When he picked up the phone the way he always did— "Yeah?"—I said, "B., I have to tell you somethin'. I'm pregnant. Tiny took me up there today." He said these simple words, "It ain't mine," and the love of my life, the pastor's son, hung up the phone on me.

I was devastated. And despite his reaction, all I could think was how much *more* I wanted to be around him. After a couple of weeks, the rumors that he was spreading about me started coming back to me. He was talkin' junk about me, saying that he wasn't my only sex partner and that my baby was not his.

Although I had not been to church in many months, if there was ever a time that I needed the Lord, it was then. I started attending my grandmother's church again. Usually in the Holiness Church, when you are unmarried and pregnant, you are not allowed to participate in the church. You can't sing in the choir or be an usher or anything that is visible. I will never forget that my grandmother didn't treat me like that. She allowed me to sing every Sunday that I was there. She knew that singing was my only saving grace. On the Sundays during my pregnancy that I didn't go to Grandma's church, I would go to B.'s father's church and sit in the back pew, with my stomach swelling with our child, trying to get some attention from him, some acknowledgment and any sign of love at all.

After church was dismissed, B. and his parents would walk right by me without saying a word to me or the child inside me. I hated myself for being in this situation. I was angry and helpless. Thoughts of dying kept running through my mind.

The stress of all of this misery caused my pregnant and frail body to fail. I was eating fast food every day, if I could afford it, and chips and candy bars on the days that I couldn't.

I thought I was going to lose my baby. I was stressin' myself out beyond belief. My spirit seemed to be telling me that there was nothing for me to live for despite the life that was struggling to grow inside of me. People were saying that my life was over because I had gotten pregnant. The whole town was talkin' about me and was disappointed in me. High Point was such a small town and, because of my grandma's church and the Barrino Family performances, we were somewhat in the spotlight.

My parents had temporarily moved to Winston-Salem, where my mother was in hell. She was without her mother, and my father was mourning the loss of his mother, Madie Barrino. When Madie died, my heart was broken again. I was the only one of the grandchildren who used to help take care of her when she was in a wheelchair.

My grandmother Madie hadn't liked my mother because she thought that she wasn't good enough for my father. Although she felt like that, she was always loving to me because of my voice. She used to say, "You bless me, chile." When I used to go visit her every week, I would wheel her outside. We wouldn't talk much, but our silent conversations meant a lot to both of us. Her death felt like another piece of me had fallen away for good.

After my grandmother Madie's funeral, while they were putting her casket into the hearse to take to the graveyard, I snuck away to the pay phone outside the church to call B. I said, "I need someone to talk to. Will you just come and talk to me?" Begging, I assured him, "you don't have to stay for long." He came a few hours later, after I had left the burial. He came every day after that. Then he started spending the nights with me. I thought he was starting to feel bad about how he was treatin' me. He was just thinkin' it was a free place to stay.

I was at a low point. I was really depressed. Only a year before I had been the most popular girl in church, everyone loved me and my voice, and now I was the bad girl who had gotten pregnant and whose life was ending. I was an outcast. My mother wasn't talking to me. My father would sometimes come and take me to the all-you-can eat restaurant, just so I could eat a solid meal. It was the worst time in my life. Everyone seemed to be looking at me and shakin' their heads. The emptiness inside caused me to simply stop trying.

I started to look different. My head hung down regularly. I had no clothes and no money. I would wear my regular jeans and, as my stomach grew, I would put a rubber band in the waistline to expand them to make room for my baby. I hadn't purchased any baby stuff, although my child was due to arrive in only a few months. The only effort I could make was to get signed up for Medicaid benefits. My mama finally went with me to do that, because she saw what a sad case I had become. I went to the doctor only a few times during my pregnancy. I was too depressed about the coming of this baby to go to the doctor every few weeks. *I was tryin' to forget*.

My family wanted me to move to Winston-Salem to be with them. My mother wanted to keep an eye on me. Winston-Salem was a slightly bigger city than High Point. I had gotten a job at a daycare in High Point at the suggestion of my grandmother.

I took a job at a local daycare in Winston-Salem. I started trying to save money for the baby. Because I was still staying out late at night, I couldn't really hold a job. Although I wasn't drinking because of the baby, I was just tired and irritable. I used to fall asleep on the kids while I was supposed to be watching them. I was working so that my baby would have things. It wasn't much, but it was all I could do.

My father was mad because I was seeing B. again. I was

happy because I thought he loved me and he had really come back. One day, he called me and said, "I need you to give me some money. I'm going to take it and make some money with it." I never asked what he was planning to do and reluctantly gave him the little money I had, thinking that by doing what he asked I was showing love. I was hoping that he would stay.

I didn't hear from B. for the next two days. He had spent all of the money. Needless to say, he didn't make anything with the money except for another good time with his friends. He didn't even think about our baby when he was spending the money. I was so hurt by his doing that with my hard-earned money that depression seized me and started to invade my heart.

I ended up having to quit my daycare job. The stress of no job and no money again led to me having problems with my pregnancy. The doctor just kept tellin' me, *You have to stop stressing or you will lose this baby.*

At home, my parents' marriage had been deteriorating for a long time. My mother was deeply involved with Addie and the church, and my father was into the ladies in the church. My father's mean streak was hurting us all. He would call me, his own daughter, "a little whore" and tell me "you are not going to be *anything*." The stress at home and the stress within caused me to have contractions that felt like premature labor, and I still had about four months to go.

I decided I had to leave my parents and this stress behind, so I went back to Tonya's and the projects. My anger at my father and his treatment of my mother and myself was causing me to feel hatred for him. I didn't want to hate my daddy. Mama begged me not to leave her. She didn't want me to leave her alone with my father. I gave her the only advice I could offer: *"You could leave, too."*

My daughter, Zion Quari Barrino, came into the world on August 8, 2001. My mom and my little eight-year-old brother, Xavier, came to the hospital. I named my daughter Zion because that is the place in the Bible where the disciples went to pray. Her middle name, Quari, was a name that I had heard somewhere and I thought it was pretty.

The girls I grew up with used to spend hours trying to create a name that they thought was unusual. Girls from the ghetto strive to give their babies unique names, like Destiny, Shanaya, and Marquita. Often that is all they have to give.

During the labor, I remember, I didn't scream. I was saying to myself, *I did this to myself.* I didn't say anything else. I just cried.

B. had come to the hospital to see me, only because I asked him to. We were sitting in silence in my hospital room, trying to figure out what to do with this baby that we didn't have a clue *what* to do with. The phone rang an hour after Zion was born. B. picked it up and it was his mother. I heard him say, like only a country boy could, "Yes, ma'am." When the time came to sign the birth certificate, Zion's daddy refused to sign. He didn't sign his own daughter's birth certificate, and his parents didn't even come see to see their granddaughter.

When I looked at Zion, all I could see was the hole in her heart that would be permanent because there was no daddy in her life. It made me so sad and all I could think about was how I was determined to fill that hole with all the things that I could provide her. First, I needed a job.

Zion and I moved back in with my parents when we left the hospital. As soon as I got home from the hospital, B.'s parents sent him away to Barber-Scotia College in Concord, North Carolina. The school is for students who want to own their own businesses. Not that B. wanted a business. He only needed a reason to walk away from us.

I didn't hear from B. for months. He never called. I was happy that my baby was in my arms. Zion was my only friend. I would look at Zion and think, What am I gonna do? I had to make a plan, but I had no answers. The only thing I could do was pray. Prayer was all I had left.

My father had started to disappear again. He was coming and going without telling anyone where he was going or when he'd be back. Sometimes he'd be gone for days at a time. It was obvious that he was involved with another woman. That is how it is where I come from. Even when folks are married there is always another woman. My mom suspected it but finally was ready to face it and speak about it. She said to me, "I think your daddy is sleeping with someone else." That is when I started hating my father.

My father finally confessed to me. He told me to my face that he was cheating on my mother. He thought he was justified in laying down with a woman who wasn't his wife because of my mother's negligence of him and her spending too much time with Addie and the church. He thought that these were valid reasons to cheat on his wife. My response to that was that I left the house and got my own apartment.

I was seventeen and my first apartment was in the First Farmington projects, the "nicer" projects on the south side of High Point. My rent was thirty dollars a week, which I could afford, and the only things I had to worry about were the telephone and the electric bills. I was able to get into the apartment because I had a child and no income. It was the projects where many baby mamas were in the same situation. First Farmington Apartments was like a camp for single, uneducated women with babies.

I started singin' to make money. It was the only thing I could do. I would sing at different churches and people would give me love offerings of cash to help support Zion and myself. My friends would sometimes give me money, too. I was survivin'—but definitely not thrivin'.

Then B. left college and moved in with Zion and me. I didn't really want him to come back since he had been no help so far, but the fantasy of being a real family stuck in my mind and I couldn't turn him away. Neither of us had steady jobs. My only "hustle" was singing at the churches. Those love offerings were all I had to pay for diapers, socks, and T-shirts for Zion. The only other help I got was WIC. WIC is a welfare program that is for baby mamas. WIC stands for Women, Infants, and Children. It provides milk, baby formula, cheese, and other food staples. WIC is set up so that you can get only a few vouchers at a time. If you run out of vouchers, you have to wait until the next month when more vouchers arrive. B. was paying into the Medicaid program. His contribution was so small that it was as if no money was coming to me at all.

My boyfriend had no problem stealing from me. He thought he was justified because his Medicaid contribution made him feel like he was supporting me. One day, I remember feeling so proud because I had a whole hundred dollars in my purse, which was for the rent and to buy food. He came into the house and said, "I need some money." I said, "No, because I need it for food." That was our first physical fight. He hit me and I hit him back. He hit me again and I hit him right back. Eventually, his hits were harder than mine, so I gave in and gave him the money. I thought that giving in to B. was coming from love. It was my "love" covering up my loneliness. I couldn't stand being lonely, so I easily forgot his "love licks." A couple of my girls in Farmington were victims of "love licks" as well. They all had reasons and excuses that made it seem okay to be hit by your man. It was a warped form of intimacy. In some way it was a privilege for the man, because he would say, "I'm the only man who is allowed to hit her." That was the thinkin' back in Farmington.

My lights were soon cut off because I couldn't pay the electric bill. B. left us again and went back to his parents' house. He wouldn't and couldn't ask his parents to help because his parents would not allow us in their house. I couldn't ask my parents for help, because it was my fault that I left them in the first place and I knew that my mama was going through her own drama with my father. B. went home to light and warmth. Zion and I were once again in darkness and cold.

I had to ask a friend, Shanetta, if Zion and I could stay with her, temporarily. Shanetta was my brother Rico's baby mama. She let Zion and me stay in her apartment. We slept on a mattress in the middle of her small living room floor. Shanetta had three children at the time.

Shanetta was struggling herself. My brother and she had gone through some terrible things. Their relationship was the talk of the Farmington Apartments. Not that it was so unusual, but because it was just the most recent incident of a woman standing up for herself. They argued a lot with each other, but mostly they were yelling and mad at themselves for ending up in a similar scenario to every war-torn relationship in each of the government-subsidized apartments.

My WIC vouchers had run out for the month. That was the month that I started stealin' milk. I would go to the store, walk the aisles, and take three cans of milk and put them in a big purse. When I needed diapers, I would go into the store, open a package of diapers, and stuff as many as I could into a purse with the milk. Three cans of milk and about ten diapers were all I needed to last me until the next WIC vouchers came. I felt bad stealin', but my baby had to eat and her daddy was not around and even when he was, he was always asking me for money or just taking what I had. Shanetta and

I, and our kids, existed on very little. All we had was each other and the daily conversation of how dirty and doggish our men had been. I would cry on her shoulder and she would cry on mine. I loved my brother, but I could almost understand her rage. It was the rage of all the women in High Point put together who had made families for these young men who so easily walked away.

My lights stayed out for a while. I wasn't going to ask anyone for the hundred dollars to get them turned back on. Everyone I knew was strugglin' and waitin' for their lights to be turned off in the next few days as well. I used to ask God in my prayers, "When is it all going to be over with?" B. was still coming over to see us. Why I let him, I don't know. I still felt like I needed him. His presence made me feel like I was better than my neighbors, because temporarily, I had my man, even if he wasn't really loving me. At least my boyfriend was *there*, and those other lost daddies were not. The fighting continued. B. would come over and fight with me and never pay any attention to Zion. When she would crawl up to her daddy, he would ignore her or act like she was a stray dog that had gotten too close to him, reminding him of obligations that he wanted so desperately to forget.

Our arguments were infecting Shanetta's fragile household, and one day, out of the blue, she gave me one hundred dollars so I could get my lights back on—and so that Zion and I could leave.

I returned to the First Farmington Apartments, apartment F in building 316, and B. moved in again. I started drinking. I would put Zion to sleep and I would go downstairs and sit on the steps and drink beer. While it was the wrong thing to do, that is what people do in the projects. Project life is like no other life. "Nothin' to do" is a common reason for the crowded staircases, beer bottles, and cigarette butts strewn throughout the parking lot. Ghetto girls need to look good, so they dress up every single day in heels, makeup, tight shorts, and halter tops. They stroll their babies up and down the walkways of the projects with their cordless phones in their pockets instead of cell phones, going as far up the block as you could go and still get reception. Sitting outside after dark was summer in the projects. The familiar sound of loud voices and deafening car radios was all you could hear inside the project's gates.

I spent too much time walkin' the projects with a drink in my hand instead of turning to God and falling on my knees. My heart had been hardened. I needed *things*, not *prayers*. I was asking myself, What was praying gonna do?

B. was always out with his friends, so I was out with mine. And when we got home, we would fight about everything and nothin' at all. We would fight because we were mad that we were sitting in the projects with no money and a child that was not conceived in true love. It continued to get worse every night.

The fights would begin when B. would get off the ugly purple couch with the stuffin' coming out. He would open the refrigerator door and yell to me that there was nothin' to eat. That would wake Zion up. I would go into the white kitchen and try to explain: "There was no money this week to get food." He would say nasty things under his breath. Things like, "How did I end up here with you?"

The morning would continue like this until B. would leave, with his last words being, "Have some food for dinner, bitch." And he would leave in a hurry.

I didn't know what to do next in my life. I tried to get back in school, but I would have had to go through social services and apply for child-care benefits. I just didn't want to go through that hassle again. They would require all kinds of paperwork and start dates and contracts and I didn't want to deal with all of that. I wasn't too good with paperwork. Besides, it was depressing going through the social services system. I felt those people's eyes were looking down on me. Their eyes said, You are a project girl. You are not going to do anything with your life. I didn't have any other options, but something in me just wouldn't allow me to go back in there and face their looks anymore. I was beginning to feel hopeless. I no longer wanted to wake up in the same life that I went to sleep in. I wanted to wake up as someone else and be somewhere else. I just had to figure out who and where I wanted to be and how I would get there.

B. and I had one last fight. Of course, we were fighting over money. When he asked for my money I said no. I told him that I was standing up for myself and for our child. This time, he knocked me out with his fist. This time he went to jail.

I wasn't going to call the police because I didn't want

him to get in trouble. It was just a "love lick," and as much as it hurt, my ego mostly, I still loved him. When B. angrily left the apartment, I immediately called my mother. My eye was swelling and blackening. My lip was busted and bleeding badly. My mother came over and called the police. My mother *made* me tell the police what B. had done to me, just like she did for me when that guy raped me. She is always the person who defends me, even when I won't defend myself.

A few hours later, B. went to the police department and turned himself in. Zion and I left our apartment and went to stay with my mama.

Mama had finally left my father and gotten her own apartment in Greensboro, a neighboring city that was only fifteen minutes away. Despite my father telling Mama that she was "useless" and "could never make it without him," she was actually living on her own. My father said that she couldn't do it, and she needed to prove him wrong. My mother found a job at a nursing home that was within walking distance from her apartment. She had no car, so she walked to work every single day.

The day after I arrived at my mama's, I was sitting in the apartment when my little brother came in, looked at my battered face, and said with a child's enthusiasm, "He messed you up!" He had a look on his face that I had never seen before. I jumped up, looked in the mirror, and crumbled at the sight. I was so ugly. My hair needed to be done. My eye was black and swollen. My lip was blue and black with trickles of blood crusted in the corners. I looked at myself and said out loud, "This ain't Fantasia! This life ain't for me! I ain't supposed to be like this!" My life was *messed up.* "I have to raise up and respect myself." I looked at Zion. She was so little and she was giving me these looks that were saying, Mama, you disgust me.

I didn't want Zion ever to see me letting a man treat me that way again. My baby wasn't going to go through it, too. My change finally was occurring. Sometimes for a change to hit you, it just takes looking in the mirror and saying what you really mean out loud.

B. was only in jail for two days. I called him when he got out and said it plain: "We have to let this relationship go or we are going to kill each other." He agreed and never came around or did anything again for Zion. When I would get weak and call him, he would hang up. He did nothing to help us. *Nothing.* I guess that's what finally gave me the eyes that I needed to see him.

Now I could see that I was in need of a better life. A couple of months after my relationship with B. had ended, I met a guy. He was a working man. His name was J.B. He was nice looking, respectful, and he told me that I was beautiful. He would ask me about Zion and he would buy her diapers when she needed them. He became like her father. He did a lot for her and he would do anything for me. He was the man I had been looking for. This was the man I needed. I thought to myself, *This* is what I should have.

After dating for four months, we moved in together. I went from having to hide my money and doing everything for myself and my child to having a man who was taking care of both of us and doing everything for me. J.B. was going to work every day and would come home at lunchtime just to bring us food. I wasn't sure that I deserved him. His generosity somehow made me uncomfortable. I wasn't used to it, and I always felt that it wasn't real and would be taken away. This happiness didn't seem real.

J.B. treated me like a queen. He is the first man who showed me what respect is.

J.B. was willing to help me financially, but he also wanted to help me help myself. J.B. wanted to help me gain my independence. He wanted to help me get my driver's license.

This was when my readin'—or the fact that I couldn't really read—came out. I told you I was not too good with paperwork, which is the real reason I didn't like going to the social services agencies. I had gotten to the eighth grade, but I had really just slid by. No one had really checked my reading comprehension, my vocabulary, or my word-recognition skills. It was easy to keep going to the next grade in public school, which wasn't good, but it was common.

When J.B. realized that I couldn't read well, he didn't laugh at me. Instead, he would show me different words on the street and in magazines and books. He would help me pronounce difficult words that I wasn't familiar with. He would buy me books and read them to me. He would make me read things to him and sound out the large words. I was ready to improve my reading. I had gotten this far without reading, and I knew that I could continue to get by in the same way. My family didn't really know that I was having trouble readin' and I didn't think they needed to know. Most people in my family couldn't read very well. So not reading was normal for us.

It only struck me that I needed to read when Zion brought over one of her books for me to read to her. I cried because I couldn't read the large words on the colorful pages of the child's book. I opened the page and recognized most of the words, but didn't know how to pronounce them. I didn't want to further humiliate myself in front of Zion. She had seen me in the worst moments, and it isn't good for a little girl to see her mother that low.

At that moment I realized that when I was trying to be cool by dropping out of school, I was at home looking stupid, not being able to read and not being able to count. I cried because the truth was that I couldn't even get a job because I was afraid that I would count somebody's money wrong. I cried because I was dumb. Plain out dumb.

I cried and knew that my tears meant that change was coming. It was time. I didn't want my daughter to come to me and ask me what I asked my mother only a few years before: "Mama, where is your diploma?" Just like my mother had to say to me, I didn't want to say to Zion, "I don't have one."

So I started attending a program to get my GED. I also returned to church. I was singing as much as I could and when I wasn't singing I was reading everything I could. I was reading street signs, signs in stores and markets, labels on groceries—I was reading everything. My relationship with J.B. continued. He was generous, loving, and kind—but still not what I really needed. God is what I needed.

As I started to listen to God, I started to become further away from J.B. It wasn't because I didn't care about him, but God's voice made me start to care about myself. I realized every day that J.B. was the person who truly had it all, and although he was givin' me a lot, I still had nothin' and would never have anything until I got up and got somethin' for myself. That is always the hardest thing when you realize something about yourself, but you have no idea how to make a change. What I realized was even though I didn't know what I was going to do, just tryin' anything would be better than sittin' scared and not movin' at all. I had a child now and needed to think about her and not think so much about myself. How would I sound tellin' Zion that I had nothin', was doin' nothin', and that my "man" was our only source of anything? Once I took the focus off me and my fear, I started thinking about this child that was here because of me and needed me to do more than just wait for someone else to take care of us. When you are in a bad spot in your life, it is easy to get so wrapped up in your situation that you can't even see your way out of it. When you stop thinkin' about yourself and think about the people around you, you will start to see the light of what you are doing and what you are not doing, just like I did.

MY MOMENT OF

FAITH: WHAT I LEARNED

And be not conformed to this world: but be ye transformed by the renewing of your mind, that ye may prove what is that good, and acceptable, and perfect, will of God.

ROMANS 12:2

- Your body is a special thing. It is a special part of you and you should never just give it away—no matter what the other girls are doing. You are a child of God and being too free with this gift of your body and your life doesn't make God happy. He will bless you when you bless yourself with self-respect.

3. Learn
from Your
Mistakes

A lot of girls I know say this, but I sure do wish I had listened to my mama. My poor mama spent so many hours trying to tell me the important things about life, and although they were all true, for some reason I thought that I needed to find out those things for myself. I remember saying to her, "I know, Mama. *I know.*" When I really didn't know anything but just thought that she was trying to scare me by making life sound harder than it is. She wasn't. *Life is hard.*

I've already told you about some of the mistakes I've made in my life. Some mistakes have already been pulled apart by all kinds of people who don't really know me and never will. Other mistakes I'm now telling about for the first time. I'm sure that people will talk all about those, too. I'm used to being talked about though, because through all of my changes I was the talk of the town around High Point. What's kind of funny is that I would say that the biggest mistakes that I have made are not the ones that you have read about, but they are the ones that almost cost me the opportunity to be the American Idol.

Even though much of my life has changed for the better, I continue to live with the consequences of my mistakes every day. One thing that the public will never know is how it *feels* to have done the things that I have done, knowing the difference between right and wrong and choosing wrong even though I now know I could have done a lot better.

The newspapers always go for the obvious: Fantasia had a baby; Fantasia grew up poor; Fantasia didn't finish high school. You already know those things, and they are easy to judge and criticize because the people who have criticized me are nowhere near as harsh on me as I am on myself. If they think some of those things are terrible, imagine living it. I figure that I should talk about it openly and honestly and hope and pray that somebody who came from a place like me, with a family like mine, with the feelings of low self-esteem and curiosity and a need to be loved will read my story and make some better choices than I did. The other thing I want to do is dig deeper and tell you in my own words what the newspapers can't or won't say.

As a child of God, I was raised to believe that God forgives as long as you give your life to Him—being "saved," it's called. I believe that because Jesus hung out with sinners and He restored them. He was able to do it for me.

My first mistake was havin' sex too early and getting pregnant. When I was sneaking out of the Wingate High School when no one was looking and running across town to meet my boyfriend at the back door of his house in the middle of the day, I thought it was fun and I felt like a grown-up. I was in charge of myself; I had people to see and things to do. When we were having sex in his childhood room on that twin bed that he had been sleeping on since he was a toddler, I just thought it was what young men do with their girl-friends.

Now, I wish I had something special to give to my husband on the day I get married. I do want to get married someday and have a real family and a daddy for Zion. *I should have waited.* Maybe I should say I should have waited until I was married, but I should have at least waited until real *love.* That love that I was feeling for B. was just "kiddie" love, as my mama always calls it. Of course, she was right. What I realized is that you can't even feel real love until you have love for yourself. What I went though with B. was far far from real love. It was real *stupid.*

Having sex when you're not an adult is not just about choosing between right and wrong. It's deeper than that. The reason I chose to allow B. to talk me into sex is because I hated myself and desperately needed to feel like someone could love me, despite my big lips and skinny body. I was willing to be talked into something that I knew was wrong—but my hunger for love and my need to bury my own hate for myself won out over sense. That's the mistake that I made, hating myself and letting those feelings of weakness rule my choices.

Having sex is not something that you do to tell your girlfriends about or to compare notes with other girls. Sex is not an activity that makes boredom go away. It's not one of those things that you could consider an accomplishment, like graduating from high school or winning a track meet. It's nothing that you should be tellin' other people. The only ones who talk about it are other girls who are doing the same wrong thing. Because I couldn't talk about it with everyone, that should have made me recognize the shame in it. Not understanding those small things was the foundation for my sexual habits. It was far deeper than bein' a church girl with nothing else to do.

I regret putting my love into B. It was a mistake, but it is one that I will never be able to reverse. He wasn't the person who was worth the valuable gift of my body. The mistake of loving B. was because I didn't love myself. Maybe if I hadn't grown up convinced that I was ugly, that my big lips were bad, and that my dark skin was a curse, I wouldn't have been chasing B. around when he was hurtin' me with every look. If I had grown up without those insecurities, perhaps I would have been able to recognize his meanness. I was so deeply insecure that I couldn't see his all-out disrespect for me.

I remember getting all dressed up to go to the mall on a

Wednesday, the day that B. was always at the mall. It took me two hours to pick out the right outfit. I wanted to be sexy. I fantasized all the way to the mall that when he saw me, he would leave all his friends and go with me. That's what I wished.

When I arrived at the mall, B. had his arm around another girl with a long ghetto name that I can't remember and long wavy hair, light skin, and thin pink lips. He looked at me from the corner of his eye as if to say, *Please keep walkin'*. He turned his head the other way and put his hand on that girl's butt. My insides were crushed. I felt sick and as if I was dyin'. I turned around and left the mall crying, blinded by the blur of my tears. All I could think was that he liked that girl better because she didn't look like *me*.

If God was punishing me for something, it was for hating myself. As children of God, how dare any of us hate ourselves.

Choosing the people that we put our love into is really important. All of the men I grew up around loved music, loved to perform, and loved to look good. They treated their women badly and they didn't respect them. And they were always looking for the next woman that they could conquer—including my daddy. Not knowin' what a good man really looks like made me choose the wrong man to love. I was wrong to think that just because B.'s father was a preacher, he would have a good heart and have respect for me. I blame myself for making a poor choice of a man and that one poor choice resulted in a lot of heartache. All I can tell you is you better find out what makes a good man. Once you know about it, you can start looking for it. The ones that look good or are "cool" may not be the ones you want. Take it from me.

As far as the sex thing goes, it was a big mistake to not listen to Mama. It is simple: we shouldn't be havin' sex without bein' married. The reason God and our mamas say that is not to deny us somethin', but to make sure that we have sex only after we have all the other things that we need *after* the sex—like havin' a man who is committed to taking care of a baby with you. Like havin' the proper education so you can make sure that the child is healthy and growin'. Like havin' a proper home that you can raise your child in. Like bein' able to show your child what a real relationship looks like between a man and a woman. These are the things that God wants for us and for our kids. Even God must be sick of seeing single mothers raise their kids without fathers, without resources, without money.

Don't get me wrong—all of my closest friends are baby mamas, so this is comin' from my heart and with no judgment. I don't want the baby mamas to continue the generational curse that my family is finally coming out of. Don't forget that my brother Rico has six children and never had a wife and he is only twenty-five. He has two baby mamas. My other brother, Tiny, is twenty-four and has two children and has never even considered marryin' his baby mama.

I understand baby mamas because I am one myself. I know you love your kids but that you usually don't love the situation you find yourself in. Havin' a baby too young with-out real financial, emotional, or psychological support is hard—it is the *hardest* thing that a young woman can do. My daughter, Zion, was not a mistake; she is a blessing. But I still should have waited to have sex, because when she was born, I would have been a bigger blessing *to her.* I didn't have any-thing to give her and because I didn't have anything to give her, my guilt makes me give her everything she wants now and that will probably make her spoiled. It is now my guilt that is feeding her along with my love. That's the truth.

My second mistake was not listening to my mama. It's a little strange to say, but in a way, I feel I was lucky to have a mother who made her own mistakes. But I still didn't listen to her. Most girls hear what they "should do" from their mothers, although their mothers sometimes have never gone through the things that they are telling them to avoid. For a young girl who thinks she's grown, it's a little hard to accept that, I know, because that's what I thought. Truth is, my mama was speakin' from her own experience with three kids and no education and a man who wasn't actin' right, and I still ignored her.

That's a mistake that I regret to this day. Think of the hardship I could have saved both my mother and me. My mother has always been open and honest with me. She told me all about sex and protection and what happens if you are raising your kids on your own. She told it all and I still wouldn't hear her. If I could tell the women and young girls just one thing, it would be this: Listen to your mamas. Listen to them for one reason only: it is *disrespectful* not to listen to them. Your mama is the person who gave you life. Your mama may not have gone through the same things that you're experiencing, but she's going to have a better idea of what *can* happen and what to avoid. If your mama hasn't gone through it herself she probably knows someone who has. A man leaving a woman to fend for herself and take care of a child is a common thing that has been happening to women for many centuries. It's not new. We didn't start it.

I am more ashamed of not listening to my mother's *silence*.

My mama has been through a lot. She has been disappointed and hurt so many times in her life. Mama wanted to be a strong person and a successful singer. She had dreams too, none of which happened for her. The fact that my mother didn't even notice that I dropped out of school; the fact that she let me go live with and run around with my thirty-year-old friends; the fact that she sensed that I was having sex and didn't say anything about it tells me that Mama had gone into a deep depression. She wasn't herself and I should have noticed, mainly because she was not really noticing me. I was watching my mother's spirit slowly dying, and I was too selfish to see and too focused on myself to say anything. I couldn't pull her out of her hole because I was too busy diggin' my own. Looking back on it, I could have been as much help to her as she tried to be to me before depression sucked her away from mothering.

When I think of all my girls in the projects who have

two and three babies, often from different men, it worries me. That is a lot of unprotected sex goin' on in the projects, and the fact that the fathers have left means that my girls and those guys never had much of a relationship in the first place. Their mistake is not their pregnancies; it was their forgetting that if they caught a disease, they wouldn't be there for their children anyway. Tears fill my eyes just thinkin' about what would happen to Zion if I got sick because of being careless with a man who was careless with me. All those times that me and my friends were together, puttin' on makeup, strapping up our high heels, and squeezing into our too-tight shorts to walk the projects, we never once mentioned diseases or death and the impact they would have on our children.

It's pretty simple, but it seems like it's really hard for us. What is so hard about sayin' no when your life is at stake? Not just your being alive, but the *quality* of your life. When you have children that you aren't ready for, all of your dreams just melt away. It's not easy being a mama who never lived her dreams, and it's not easy looking at one.

But I don't blame myself anymore, because in those days, I thought my life was nothing to protect. It seemed that death was something that happened often enough that everyone around me had almost lost the fear of it. The aftermath of death was something that we got used to. Being from the ghetto changes your feelings about life and death. Death is just something that happens to people when they're not lookin'. The news of death is just something new to do when the boredom gets to be too much. The news of murders, car accidents caused by drunk drivers, gangs and drug overdoses travels around town fast like the news of how big the lottery was that week. Funeral arrangements and telling the whole town are all "somethin' to do" for people who never have nothin' to do. When the funeral is over and the excitement of death has died down again, everyone returns to what they were doing before. At least for that short period, life around death was exciting. With that as a backdrop for my life and for so many young bored people in America, life is not such a big deal. Being careless with life just seemed like what everyone did.

My third mistake was dropping out of school. That was my biggest mistake ever, and I pay for it every day. You see, I'm what I would call a functionin' illiterate. That means that I "get by" in life, but my readin' isn't what it should be. *I am workin' on it.* I am still not confident enough with words or letters. If I see a word that I'm not familiar with, I still get *scared.* Sometimes I don't even know how to begin to pronounce them or even how to sound the letters out. Not a day goes by that I'm not ashamed about my situation. If you hand me a newspaper, I just look at the pictures and try to figure out what happened. I do recognize the common words like "death" and "money," "taxes," "president," "baby," "marriage," and "rich," but most big words or too many words together just scare me. I know that this is a shock. This is one of those private mistakes that will no longer be private once this hits the news. That is why when I sign my autograph I draw my lips. When people ask me to write a special message, I have trouble forming words right on the spot, so I write something short like "Be Blessed" or something like that, something that I already know how to write. Whatever I write, I mean it from my heart.

Although I got to ninth grade, I forgot a lot of things. I had never made good grades except for that one time in Charlotte, when I actually sat and listened to what the teachers were saying, but that was a long time ago. It was the only time that I wasn't distracted with dreams of B. cloudin' my brain. I know that I'm smart. I'm just not *educated*. I used to say that I was never blessed with "smarts." But I feel differently now. I'm blessed with "smarts" because I haven't given up and I will learn to read all of the words there are to read someday soon. That is my promise to myself.

You must think I'm crazy to put my business out here like this, but the reason I'm doing this is to go behind the gossip and let you know that this is one mistake that *no one* should ever make. *Ever.* In those days, when I was thinkin' I was being cool by not going to school, I didn't realize that the coolest part of my life should have been spending my days at Montlieu Elementary School. A Laurin Welborn Middle School, and T. Wingate Andrews High School. The coolest part of my nights should have been struggling with math homework and writing papers. Most of my friends were actually going to school and learnin' somethin', and I was at home lookin' stupid—watchin' TV, not being able to read, not being able to count. In those days, I didn't even feel comfortable counting.

Truthfully, I never applied for many jobs, because I couldn't fill out the application. Whenever I tried, I left so many questions blank because I couldn't read them that the applications always ended up in the garbage. That is dumb, *plain out dumb*. This is how you see that one big mistake just creates another one. It's a chain reaction.

I was embarrassed and ashamed and I still am, despite the *Idol* competition, despite the pictures in magazines, despite my improved self-esteem. I was stupid for not stayin' in school. And the private part of my shame is that I want to be as smart as everyone else. I want to be wise about my own money, I want to be able to understand a contract that's presented to me and not have to ask someone else what it means. I want to be able to read a script and take it home and think about it on my own time instead of needing someone to go through it with me. I want to be able to think for myself and not have to walk around with people all the time, helping me get through the simplest things. My public mistake is that I didn't finish school. My private mistake is that, although I'm talking about it now for the first time, I'm ashamed and hating myself for my choices. I'm angry that my life brought me to this place. I'm angry that my parents couldn't control me better. I'm angry that I have already missed opportunities in my life. Although my readin' thing makes a good story, the real story is how I have managed to fool the world into thinking that I could read. The real story is how Hollywood and show business wouldn't want the world to know that illiteracy is a real thing that affects a lot of young people, like me. It is one of those ugly things that no one wants to talk about, yet keeping a secret just makes a new generation of illiterates. This why so many young kids don't have jobs—they can't read a job application. They are not lazy and ghetto, which is what everyone says about us. Is that what they are saying about me? Or are they not saying that because I'm a singer? Is the public image more important than what is really goin' on with me? Instead of getting a free car, what I could have used was a tutor—but that would have meant that choosing me as the American Idol was their mistake.

I don't want anyone to lose faith in me, but I decided to be honest so that all of the other young people like me will know in advance what droppin' out of school really turns into. My life looks like a fairy tale in many ways, but you have to remember that life is not a fairy tale. I'm the American Idol, which seems like a fairy tale, but I can't even read a fairy tale to my four-year-old daughter.

While I'm tellin' the truth and admittin' things, I should tell you that I don't even have a driver's license. J.B. was trying to help me get one, but the real work of learning how to drive and knowing the rules of driving, I had to do for myself. I didn't even know where to start. When I won the car on *Idol*, they handed me the keys as soon as I stepped off the stage. I was filled with mixed emotions of joy, pride, and the fear of someone finding out that I couldn't drive. I was afraid that they would take the car away. I was also filled with dread because holding those keys in my hand meant that it was really time for me to learn to read in order to get the driver's license and to be able to live this new life that was right before me, that I was holding in my hand. I knew right then that I would have learn to read before I could really enjoy this blessing of having my own car.

In the midst of all of the excitement and rush of being the American Idol (like having to complete an album right away), I still have not had the time to learn all that I need to learn in order to get my driver's license. I gave the Ford Focus to my mother, who had never had her own car. I bought myself another car, which I let everyone else in my family drive for me. If you can imagine that—I didn't even get to test-drive my own car, because I didn't have a license. My cousin, Angelica (we call her "Boo Boo" because her mother was called "Boo" and so she came to be known as "Boo Boo"), test-drove the car, with me in the passenger's seat. I asked her, "Does it ride well?" Boo Boo said, "It's a smooth ride." I said to the salesperson who was in the backseat, "I'll take it." If I had stayed in school I would be test-drivin' my own car. I would be arguin' with the press when they misquote me. I would have been able to say somethin' "smart" to Simon Cowell when he said somethin' "smart" to me. I am missin' out on that stuff.

On that day when I actually did try to get my driver's license, the man looked at the mostly blank written test when

I turned it in, and said, "Ma'am, go home and *study*." He didn't know that I had never learned how to study.

My fourth mistake was turning my back on God. When I needed God most, I completely gave up on Him. I was going through so many things and I felt like He wasn't listening anymore. It wasn't God's fault. He was putting me through these trials and I was doing these things to myself. God could see that I needed to be woken up and brought back to Him. And this is the positive thing about making mistakes. If you do believe that God has a plan for you, while you are going through hard times, you can always know that His plan includes you learning the things that you *need* to learn. Your pain is just God's reminders and they get *louder and louder*.

God has successfully brought me back to Him and to my senses. But now, I worry that by tellin' it all to the world, people might think badly of my parents. My parents did the best they could with what they had to work with. They taught us manners and the difference between right and wrong and to give our lives to God. Being raised in High Point was just a bad startin' point, and so what happened happens to most families like ours: too many mouths to feed, too many children havin' children, not enough money to feed them all, and a million dreams that never get off of Interstate 85.

Some people would say that it's a mistake to tell my story like I am. I can just hear the ladies from the church sayin', "I can't believe that girl put her business out in the street shamin' her family like that." I can just hear them! But what they don't understand, or maybe they will someday, like the Bible says, is that "the truth shall set you free." And by getting all of this out of my mind and having it stop weighing heavily on my heart, I can finally begin to mend all of my mistakes.

Anyone who thinks that I should not be putting my business out should remember that it is just as hurtful to be the topic of a High Point porch conversation as it is to be on page 20 of a *tabloid* with a made-up story about how I don't speak to my father. What happens in every person's life is private and up to the people who are livin' it, not up to the people who are talkin' about it to decide what is what. If anything, we should be there to help each other and prop each other up when we're fallin' down.

Today, the only thing left to do after acknowledging my mistakes and learning from them is to move on. I have to move on for Zion. All young mothers have to move on and be the best mothers that we can be and not dwell on our mistakes. Our babies are a blessing. Truth is, our children are here now and they don't want to live in the shadow of our mistakes. It's our job to make life bright, finally.

I want Zion to have all the things that I couldn't have. I want her to love her own life. I want her to feel happiness all around her. I want her to have the vision of what she wants in her own head so she is not influenced by anything that she sees that someone else is doing. I want her to focus on God. I want her to be involved in sports because that will give her discipline. My main focus is her schoolin'. I want to see my baby graduate from high school and go to college. When I'm gone, I want to know that she can depend on herself, because she will be educated. Zion is smart. *She* can do it.

I also want her to carry herself with respect. I don't want her to make any of the mistakes that I made. Of course, all mothers want this! I want her to experience the things that I didn't get to experience when I was younger. I don't want her to learn these things when it's too late. Not after the fact, like both my mother and I did.

I want for Zion to be able to stand up for herself in relationships with men. I want Zion to be around good male role models. I want her to grow up around men who are married and love their kids and their wives. I want Zion to know how to pick a man for herself. My dream is that Zion will never let a man yell at her or put his hands on her. My dream is that the man in her life wouldn't even think about that. In a relationship, I want Zion to look for a man who can be her friend and prayer partner. I hope that she meets a man who will never cheat on her. I don't want her to accept a man cheating on her as normal like many women do, including my own mother.

I wanted Zion to be able to say, "I didn't see my mom go through abuse." But she did, and now it's up to me to paint a different picture in her mind. I want Zion to be a woman who demands respect. I want Zion to be a truly strong woman—not just look like one.

I figure that the best way for Zion to learn all these things is for me to live them myself. I have made a lot of changes. I had to. I had to change the type of men that I was interested in. Now I'm working so hard on my career in music, I want a man who is also business oriented, someone who is *serious*. I look back and see a very different me and I can really see how much I have changed by how my idea of the man for me has changed. I used to be into guys who were thugs. I liked men with their pants hangin' low and who were showin' the bling-bling. I liked men who ran the streets all day, accomplishing nothin' but seemin' busy. That turned me on! Now I want an educated, righteous man. A man who looks good as well as a man who has respect for himself, for others, for me and my baby. I need someone who has some common sense and someone who prays when common sense is not enough. These days I want a man who works and who had a dad or a solid role model in his life who taught him how to treat a woman. That is what I really need in my life: someone who was raised right. Now, when I see some guy with his pants down to his ankles, all I can say is "Pull your pants up!"

I'm trying my best to correct my mistakes. I have this incredible chance to change my life and I have my whole life ahead of me. I have started reading and writing at every opportunity I get. I have a lot of people who love and support me and understand why I might not know some things that they know. They even help to push me a little further. And every day, I feel my confidence grow just a little because I know a little more today than I knew yesterday. Now that is real news! I am trying to get my GED and my driver's license. I am blessed to have my music give me so much, but as I work to write this book and tell my story, I know that my education just started.

After all, I was raised right. I just *chose* to be wrong.

MY MOMENT OF
FAITH: WHAT I LEARNED

"For with the heart man believeth unto righteousness: and with the mouth confession is made unto salvation."

ROMANS 10:10

- It's always good to listen to somebody. Listen and learn. You don't know everything even when you think you do. I should have listened to people who have been living much longer than me.
- I have learned that prayer does change things.
- I have learned to take my negatives and turn them into positives.
- I have learned that I can do anything I want if I put my mind to it.
- I have learned to let go of the negative; it is irrelevant to me right now. I am becoming a strong woman.
- I have learned how to be strong. I have learned not to care what people are sayin', as long as I'm making a difference in my life. That's all you have to do—try—to make a difference.

4. Never Give Up

"**G**irl, you need to do something *right* for the first time." My grandmother's hard words lingered in my mind. She was right. I needed to get out of my haze, get back with God, and continue my search for my gift, whatever it was. The problem was, I didn't even know how to begin or where to look. The time I spent being invisible, hiding behind self-pity, had become a bad habit. It was especially hard because most of my family was in some sort of a haze—either in a drug haze, a smoke haze, or just a plain depression haze. I have been surrounded by people growing up who have had their struggles with drugs and alcohol. Family photos always show the adults in my family with a bottle of beer in their hands or a cocktail, as my aunts used to call those mixes of juice and alcohol.

When we kids would ask for a sip, my aunts would always say this is "adult juice." Everyone's eyes were red and they all had cigarettes in their hands. When we would pose for pictures with our aunts and uncles, the smell of their hot alcoholic breath would burn our noses, making us want to grow up so we could smell just like them.

Smoking was glamorous back then, and it was especially glamorous in the ghetto, where it seemed luxurious because you had to *pay* for it, which meant you had some money. Smoking was a sign of maturity when I was comin' up.

Although I didn't have a real plan for my life, I knew I wasn't going there—or at least not that far. I had some dreams that I had not yet figured out how to accomplish, but I had dreams. My dreams came from watching the people on the television with their fancy new cars and their big houses. I knew that people who sang could have those things, and I was always amazed that my aunts and uncles who sang didn't have those things.

Yes, I had smoked a little, but not when I was pregnant and not often because of my voice. Everyone else around me sang and smoked, so I thought, by comparison, that I wasn't that bad. B. started me drinking, and I did drink too much sometimes, but there are no pictures of me in those days. All my friends in the projects were always posin' for pictures, showing all the "good times" we had. I never wanted to be in those pictures. I didn't want that to be how I was remembered.

A lot of people had been suggesting that I try out for

American Idol. They all kept saying it. My father's sister, Aunt Sheryl, and J.B. were pushin' it the most. Aunt Sheryl had called me and told me about Kelly Clarkson, saying, "There is a white girl who can really *sing*! And then there is a guy named Ruben who is fat but he's really good, too!" It went on and on and on. Everyone was talking about this TV show that I had never seen. My aunt Sheryl sounded so excited, it was as if these *American Idol* victories were personal victories. Seeing all of those young people succeeding with music, I guess, reminded her of me and my big voice that was wastin' away in High Point, North Carolina, only heard by churchgoers and wedding and funeral guests.

Aunt Sheryl talked about all those singers like she knew them personally, and I didn't even know what she was talkin' about. I kept wonderin', What is this *American Idol*?

J.B. did more than talk about it. He came home with all the information about the competition, the upcoming auditions, and the seven cities they were going to that year. One of the cities was Atlanta, which was only four hours away. J.B. knew I could get to that one. Suddenly, this thing called *American Idol* seemed more possible than I thought. I was curious about it, since the only thing that was needed was that you sing, and that I could do, without any fear. For once, I could do something without any help from anyone.

My family had never watched the show on television. All we knew was that my aunt Sheryl and J.B. had watched it and recommended it and we trusted them. So I went to my brother Rico and said, "Let's go to this audition. I want you to take me." Rico is a singer, too, and he plays bass and drums and he has a natural talent for arranging music. He has a great "ear," as my father used to say. He has always been interested in auditioning for anything that would get him into the limelight and out of High Point, so he was the perfect driving companion.

As always, we had no money between us, so my grandmother gave us money for gas and Daddy gave us eatin' money. My mother offered to watch Zion while I was gone. My mother didn't realize what it would mean, so she offered to take care of Zion without even thinking about it. Now she jokes with me that she never thought I would even get into the competition, so she thought she was only going to have Zion over that one weekend.

A couple of weeks later, Rico and I were ready to head to Atlanta, Georgia. I walked around the house with a new sense of purpose. *I was going to a singing competition.* I was practicing my Aretha Franklin tone and my Patti LaBelle riffs and my Ella Fitzgerald scats and my own dance and church moves. My mother feared privately that I was setting myself up for a major disappointment, so she just walked around shaking her head gently.

The drive to Atlanta was pleasant because with Rico and me, it's always jokes. We make fun of each other, imitate each other, and sing songs from the radio together. Other times we just talk about our family and our kids. We would always laugh at the stories that our uncles and aunts told us about drinkin' and all the crazy things they used to do. The whole family thought those stories were so funny, and so Rico and I told them again and again. It was harder to tell them without acting them out, but we did the best we could while driving and being confined in our seatbelts. Other times during the drive, I would tell Rico stories about Zion and the cute things she would say and the way she would hang around my neck because she never wanted to be away from me, even when I was just going to the store.

When we arrived in Atlanta, we drove straight to the Georgia Dome. We were excited just to be a part of something so huge. The Dome seats seventy-five thousand people. All we knew about the Georgia Dome was that it's where the Atlanta Falcons play football. When we arrived the first night at the Dome, I was shocked by how many people there were. Rico and I had no idea of the magnitude of this competition. They were auditioning seven thousand people in Atlanta that day alone. People had begun lining up two days before because they thought it was important to be the first in line. Most people don't realize that Kelly Clarkson and I were both the last to audition in our cities. Being first means nothing at all.

The way that the audition was set up was that everyone was sleeping on the floor of the Georgia Dome on the concourse level, waiting on their chance to sing.

When we got to the building seven thousand people were singing, sleeping, talking on cell phones, and making sure that they looked good. There were beautiful black girls with long legs, big voices, and perfect teeth. There were handsome guys trying to be the next D'Angelo or Maxwell with their hair in braids and Afros and locks. They wore nice shirts and sunglasses to make them extra cool. There were gorgeous blondes, brunettes, and redheads. They had blue eyes, green eyes, and eyes that were dark as night. There were short girls, fat guys, even singing twins. I had never seen so many people in my life, and I could never have imagined that that many people thought they were singers. I was confident because those years singing' in church choirs made me know that my voice was big and that people really loved to hear me sing. I was just overwhelmed that the world was so big and that so many people also thought that they could sing.

The morning of the audition was spent getting people into the building and into the bleachers in the stadium. Once we were seated, there was a huge TV screen that showed the images taken by a giant camera scanning the audience from overhead, showing how large the crowd really was. There were a lot of production assistants, which I learned meant anyone who was associated with the show but did all kinds of things, from little jobs like getting coffee to big jobs like trying to control a crowd of seven thousand desperate singers.

Someone on the production staff was giving us instructions and information about when the auditions would actually start and what to do in the meantime. The way that it was set up was that people could come and go as they pleased once they were checked in. There was a door on one side for entering the Dome and another door for leaving the Dome, in order to control the traffic flow and avoid the press. The production staff wanted to make sure that the press didn't get any footage before the show aired. The production staff was also afraid that people who were told that they should go home, based on their audition, would then leave the stadium and try to come back in to audition again.

It was February in Atlanta, and so it was actually warm outside and sunny enough that people wanted to go outside. On the official Web site of *American Idol* they had mentioned what we could bring and what we couldn't. They suggested sleeping bags, folding chairs, and water. The Dome also had a menu especially for all the aspiring singers, like Rico and me, who only had enough money to get there. The two-dollar burger special and the one-dollar nachos special that they offered was all we could buy, and we were appreciative that they had anything on the menu that we could get.

Rico had forgotten his identification, so I was the only one who could audition. I stayed with Rico for a minute after he realized that he had left his ID in his other pants. He was very upset but trying hard not to show it. Because I'm his sister and I know him so well, I knew that he was near tears, but don't ever tell him that I told you that.

I went up to the registration desk and received the number that would be my new name throughout the competition. I was hoping that I would make it far enough that they would use the number a lot. My number was 34572.

There were three rounds of auditions to be held out on the enormous football field. Across the field there were about twelve tables with three judges at each table. There

were three lines of singers in front of each table. The producer at each table was responsible for the initial selection.
This selection process was just to narrow down the number
of contestants. These producers are not musicians, they are
TV people, so this initial round was just to create a group
that would be ready for the executive producers to see. It
looked like the other thing that these producers were doing
was looking for talented singers as well as not-so-talented
singers, but ones who would make good television. These
auditions are the ones that you see on the outtakes of the audition process. It made me sad when I heard that they take
some people just for the sake of making good TV, but then
again, I'm not a producer and I have no idea what makes
people watch a TV show. They must know what they are
doing. With seven thousand people and only twelve hours,
the first comments to the people auditioning were very brief.

There were two auditions before you actually got to sing
in front of Randy Jackson, Paula Abdul, and Simon Cowell,
the show's main judges. I was slightly nervous because there
were so many people auditioning. All of them were practicin'
and warmin' up their voices as well as primpin' and makin'
sure that they looked good. I was just happy to be there. I
was just happy to be doing *something*. I really hadn't had
time to consider how I looked or what I was wearing. I had
been removed from the real world for so long that just getting there was a big deal and figuring out what to wear never
really crossed my mind.

I was wearing a pair of tight jeans, a pair of black boots with high heels that I usually wore with my shorts in the projects, and a T-shirt with revealing holes in it. Three people at a time went up to individual microphones to be heard, each by a different producer. I went up and sang the classic Stevie Wonder song "Signed, Sealed, Delivered." The producer listened to me and said, "You are going to the next round." And that was that. I was expecting a little more from him considering the distance that I traveled and how important I thought that being on that show was.

I was relieved to have made it to the next round, but restless and needed to get out. After all, we were in Atlanta. Rico and I decided to go to the karaoke area that they had set up downstairs with the snack bar. We relaxed and had some fun. We hadn't been too nervous about the audition, I guess because with so many singers there, I figured in the back if my mind, like my mother had, that I wouldn't make it anyway. Rico and had made a serious bet in the car: If Rico won the competition, I would sing backup for him, and if I won, he would sing backup for me. Because he couldn't audition, my audition would determine what the both of us would be doing with our future.

Rico and I started to dream. If you win, we'll stay in hotels and order room service, he would say. And I would say if I win, I'll be able to buy Zion all the teddy bears in the world. And Rico would say, If you win, you can buy us all a mansion, and I said, If I win, I will buy Mama some clothes.

And Rico would say, If you win, I will be your bodyguard and backup singer on tour. And the dreams just kept going and going, growing and growing.

After we returned from singing karaoke, an older black security guard called me over and said, "I heard you singing. I suggest that you take the pierce out of your lip. You would be much prettier without it." He looked like my uncle Jute, so I said, respectfully, "Yes, sir, I'll do that." People say I am old-fashioned to refer to people as "ma'am" and "sir," but that is the country way in which I was raised, and it is one thing that was easy to remember and even easier to do. "Sir" and "ma'am" go a long way where I'm from.

The piercing was just one of the things I had done because I was so bored. I had gotten it when I saw an advertisement for a piercing place. I just went in there to ask about it, and I ended up having them pierce my face, just over my top lip. Someone in the piercing place recommended that I get the piercing exactly in the same place where Marilyn Monroe's mole was, right above her lip.

Rico and I didn't want to spend the night on the floor of the Georgia Dome, and our cousin, Junebug, lived in Atlanta. We decided to go over to his house, eat, and then come back early in the morning so we could at least get a good meal and a good night's sleep. The next morning we arrived back at the Dome to find that the doors had been shut. *Locked.* The guards had been instructed to not let anybody else into the building. There were too many people in the Dome, and the producers were worrying about how they were going to keep order when so many people were coming in and going out.

There were about a hundred people outside the Georgia Dome, cryin', cussin', and yellin' at the security guard, who just kept sayin', "No one else is getting in." We all had been told that we could get back in that morning, but no one expected it to be so many people, I guess. The scene was a mess. Everyone else was carryin' on, and I just started cryin' to myself and prayin'. I prayed aloud, "Lord, if you can get me in that door, I will change my life." I prayed, but we still were not gettin' in. Rico and I left the Dome with all of those dreams draggin' behind us like a torn tail.

I cried all the way to the car, and once I got into the car, I pulled out a cigarette to calm my nerves. I had been smoking for a couple of years. It was what I saw all the people around me doing to "calm their nerves." I needed one at that moment, so I picked up my pack of cigarettes. We got back to Junebug's house, and I called home to tell my family what had happened. Everyone at the house said, "Go back!" I told my mother, "I'm not going to make myself feel even worse by bein' turned away a second time." Sadly, I said, "It just wasn't meant to be." I hung up the phone slowly and almost before the call had disconnected, Daddy was calling us back and saying, "Go back to that Dome! Go back! You hear me, you go back!" That force in his voice brought me right back to all the years that his voice made me shiver with the excitement of having a real daddy in our house. That presence that he always had was still there after all those years. Not wanting to disappoint my father, Rico and I did as we were told. We even said, "Yes sir!" Rico and I drove back to the Dome.

We went back, and the security guard from the night before who mentioned my lip piercing saw me and motioned for me to come to the door. He said, "Did you audition yet?" and I said, "No," and he said, "I've got to get you in there." He went back in and came back out with one of the producers from *American Idol*. All those thousands of people had gone home, and I was the last person to get into the building. And I was the one who wasn't supposed to get in at all.

The judges were exhausted. I had prayed on this and this was my last chance—for everything. I walked onto the football field. There were twelve tables lined up on the field with three judges at each table: a producer and two production assistants. It was at the end of the day, and the Georgia sun was setting slowly. I walked up to the microphone, introduced myself, and sang Roberta Flack's "Killing Me Softly." I felt confident and started to feel the emotion of the song and ignored the fact that there were two other contestants singing at the same time in front of the other tables nearby. I could feel my three producers listening to me. I was in my own world. The producer simply said, "Fantasia, you are going on to the next round." I wanted to shout, but all I said was, "Oh my God, God, I thank you. God, I thank you."

I ran to Rico. He hugged me and we went back to the car. The pack of cigarettes was sitting on the passenger seat. I looked at them, considered having one in celebration, and then threw the whole pack out of the window. I had made a promise to God and He had kept His promise to me.

Two weeks later, everyone came with me for the next round of auditions. This audition was not in the Dome; it was in a building in downtown Atlanta called Americas Mart. It's a large warehouse about thirteen stories tall. This is a building that showcases art exhibits and flea markets. This set of auditions was held on two floors of the industrial building. I went to the registration desk and got my number. I was nervous this time. All of the "beautiful girls" were there with their outfits and their long hair and light skin. I was not feeling confident. All those feelings of ugliness that I had when I was in school—I was too dark skinned, big lipped, and skinny—came over me. The beautiful girls were flippin' their hair and flauntin' their boobs. I just knew one of them would win. Girls like that are *idols*. I was just a good singer.

There were two parts of this audition, and it was held over two days. The first day the contestants waited in a room that was on one of the lower floors of the building. That was called the holding room. Two contestants were taken up at a time to perform in front of the executive producer and more production assistants. Five contestants were taken from the holding room to be "on deck." I didn't know what a holding room was, but I figured it meant that it was almost my turn. Those five contestants waited on the five folding chairs outside of the audition room door. This audition required that you have a nicer outfit than the last. J.B. bought me an outfit.

It was nice, but it was nothing compared to what the other girls had on. Some looked like they had already become the American Idol.

I wasn't really sure what I was going to sing. I had practiced a couple of different songs. I worked on songs by Mary J. Blige, Aretha Franklin, Natalie Cole, and Tina Turner. Tina jumped into my spirit, and because I was needing confidence that day, I sang her classic, "Proud Mary." Once I started singin', I felt strong and energetic. I was "rollin'," just like the song says. After I sang, the producer said, "Fantasia, you are beautiful. I love your name. You are the one." The judge pointed his finger at me and repeated, "Fantasia, you are the one."

The next day was the big one. I was going to sing for the folks you see on TV—record producer Randy Jackson; recording artist Paula Abdul; and record executive (and infamously nasty man) Simon Cowell.

While watching the contestants in front of me, I listened to the answers they were giving in response to the simple question "Why do you think you should be the next American Idol?" Everyone was talkin' all over themselves, saying dumb things like, "I have worked so hard and I have been singing all my life and that's why I should be the American Idol!"

I decided I wasn't going to say anything like that, because the judges were bored of hearing it over and over again. I walked up to the mic and said, "My name is Fantasia Barrino. I have a two-year-old daughter; her name is Zion.

My lips are big, but my talent is bigger." The judges were shocked that I was so bold to say what everyone was thinking about my lips. They laughed nervously but didn't know how to respond, so they asked me about my child. One of them said, "You have a child?" I said, "I do," and they asked, "What are you going to sing, Fantasia?" I sang a Marvin Gaye song, "I Heard It Through the Grapevine," and Simon said, "Fantasia, you are going to Hollywood."

My whole family—my mama, my daddy, J.B. Grandma Addie, and Zion—were all waiting in the hallway, givin' me so much love and kisses when I came out of that audition. We were all takin' pictures and smiling like folks who had never smiled before. It was all a blur. It was amazing how life can change in one moment. Suddenly, I had hope.

Out of the 42,000 contestants who were seen in seven cities, 117 were going to Hollywood. When we arrived in Holly-wood, we were placed in a hotel near the Pasadena Civic Center, where we were going to perform. I had never been to Pasadena before. I had never been to California for that mat-ter. The sky was so blue it looked fake. The palm trees tow-ered over everything, and it felt like I was walking through a cloud. I prayed for God to keep me from burstin', I was so excited.

We were immediately given a roommate. My roommate was the same age as me and she was female. That was the cri-teria for roommate selection. My roommate partied the whole time. All of this stuff had happened so fast to me. I was having to deal with so many people and all these person-alities. It was all new to me. Back home, everyone was the same. I was seeing and dealing with types of people that I had never even imagined before. It was exhausting. I couldn't even think about partyin'. I just needed to get my rest and tune out this whole week of auditions. Every day after I did whatever I needed to do for *Idol*, I would go back to the hotel, call my family, say my prayers, and go to sleep.

I heard one of the producers call this week "boot camp." It was crazy. This was the time that the producers could see who had real talent, not just people who could sing in the shower.

The first audition you can pick any song you want and sing it alone. That was simple enough. I chose another R&B classic that my mother used to sing around the house, and I knew it well after hearing it for years on end. The song was called, "I Try" by Angela Bofill. The song was all about lovin' a man who doesn't love you. I sang the song, remembering everything my mother and I had been through. My heart felt every note.

For the second audition, you had to write a song on your own. I can't even remember what I came up with, but it was soulful and allowed me to show my "big vocal," as my mother calls it. I was getting the swing of this process, and it was feeling easier to me. I was reaching my comfort zone. I was singin'! Although the number of contestants was now only 117, there was still craziness. Managing all of the audi-tions, comments, judges, and egos was a lot to handle. Most of the days were spent auditioning at the Pasadena Civic Center, practicing for the next round's assignment, or at the hotel, trying to prepare your clothes for the next audition. Because *American Idol* is a TV show, everything about the process is being taped. Everywhere you look there is a camera in your face. During the aired season, often clips of the audition process are shown, especially if the people make it to the Top 12, which is when the professional stylists and makeup artists start working with the singers. Before that, we had to do our own hair and makeup, which is scary, especially if you have never been on camera before and don't know how you'll look. Some of the people that I was competing against were from New York City and Atlanta. Those people know about fashion and clothes. They know how to make themselves look good. They compete against other people every day. I didn't feel like I had looked good for the past three years, since before I had gotten pregnant.

Just like the producer said, those auditions were like singin' boot camp. Instead of being told to do push-ups at a moment's notice, you were asked to perform a particular style of song that has to be prepared in less than a day. Sometimes these songs are performed in a group and other times you are asked to sing a solo. You have to be ready to do whatever they ask. It helps to have lots of different kinds of songs in mind because you have very little time to learn anything. The folks who know lots of different styles of music have a better chance. Because I had been singing in church my whole life it wasn't that hard for me to put on a smile or make people shiver with a song. That is what church singin' is all about. Also, because I grew up around so much music, I knew lots of songs and lots of styles. The different singing assignments were my push-ups.

After the first day, I started seeing people messin' up. They just weren't ready for this kind of singin' on demand. That made me feel bad for them and scared for myself at the same time. I knew I could do it, but you never knew what would make the judges eliminate you and send you home. We were expected to do some sort of an audition every day of this first week, and every day people were cryin' and goin' home. Even when we weren't auditioning we were being watched by all of the producers who were checking out our vibe, checkin' to see if your spirit was in the wrong place, and makin' sure that you weren't catty and unprofessional. I saw girls sent home for not remembering their lyrics, guys messin' up with their harmonies in the group exercises. One girl was sent home because she wasn't "connecting with the audience." The producer told her, "You can't be a performer if you aren't connecting with the audience. You have to go home."

After each audition, whether it was a solo or a group piece, we would have about a twenty-minute break to eat or get something to drink. Then you were paired up for your next assignment, whether it was with a vocal coach for solos or with other singers for your group assignment. What was so hard about all of this for me was all these TV folks barking orders because everything is moving so fast, telling me what to do and where to be. I wasn't used to people who took their work so serious and knowing exactly what they wanted. I didn't know how to take them sometimes. I couldn't even joke with them to calm my own nerves, so I just listened as hard as I could and did what they said. And I kept seeing a steady line of people going home every day.

After 6:00 p.m., officially, we were free, but we usually used that time to practice some more or we could go out with the new friends that we had met. I never went out. I was too nervous that I would oversleep the next morning or forget what I was supposed to do or forget where I was supposed to be early in the morning. I had to work *hard* to concentrate. I hadn't concentrated so hard since the eighth grade. I don't think I ever concentrated before, really. I was having to listen to directions twice as hard to hear what the producers were sayin'. There were so many different room numbers and times and group numbers, I was scared all the time that I would mess up by not showing up or going to the wrong room at the wrong time and be sent home.

One day we got a half day to go shopping. It was time for the last set of auditions before the final cut to thirty-two people. My roommate asked me if I wanted to go with her, but I had no extra money and Mama didn't send me with a credit card, so I told my roommate that I had to practice something for my solo at the end of the week. I went to my room and cried, knowing that I didn't belong in this fancy competition with all these people who could go shopping when they wanted. I didn't belong in this competition because if they didn't make it, they had something else that they could do with their life. This was all that I had for my life.

I just kept wearin' my same pair of tight jeans with different tight tops and different big hoop earrings and matching high-heel shoes. But when I sang, I just sang from my heart and my voice probably sounded better than those jeans looked, but the music was my gift from God and I was finally sharing it with the world. It was in those moments that I knew whatever happened, it was gonna be okay.

On one audition, we were partnered with another contestant and we were told we had to learn a Supreme song. My partner and I picked the classic "Where Did Our Love Go" I remembered every word from growing up in our music-filled household. It was an easy choice for me. I made it through to the next round, but my partner didn't. Even though singers were partnered up, they were still looking at us as individuals. They just wanted to see how our voices blended with other voices and if you could harmonize. The last song I sang before the cut was made to thirty-two contestants was "Something to Talk About." With this song, I went in a totally different direction from everyone else. Most people were choosing contemporary songs from urban or pop radio. My song was not on any urban or pop radio station I had ever heard, and it was really different, because it was Bonnie Raitt. The song was sassy and unique, especially for me, and it used my voice in a special way. I remember

Simon Cowell struggling with his critique, but finally saying, "You're different, Fantasia. *I like that.*"

That is what God has been trying to tell me.

The first week in Hollywood, 117 contestants turned into 32.

For the next four weeks, the group of 32 is broken into four groups of 8. Each group of 8 will return to Hollywood for a separate week to do another mini boot camp. My group was Diana DeGarmo, Jennifer Hudson, Marque Lynche, Matthew Metzger, Ashley Thomas, Erskine Walcott, and Katie Webber and me. This was Group One, so I stayed on for another week.

For this week, each of us had our own room. Finally, I had plenty of quiet time to pray and really understand what was happening to me and around me.

I felt myself getting stressed during this week when I should have been happy that I had made it that far. The auditions were not what was stressin' me. The real hurdle during this part of the auditions was that things started being said about me on the Internet. The *American Idol* Web site is one of the most visited sites on the Web, and the viewer chat rooms are a favorite feature. The entertainment press follows the *American Idol* process as closely as possible. Once I had made it into the Top 32, stories about my child and the fact that I didn't finish high school started breaking. That made me mad. I couldn't be the only person out there who didn't finish high school. What was the big deal? It was my business, not theirs. They were saying that I was "ghetto" and a "ho" on the chat lines. It wasn't anything that I hadn't heard before, but the weird thing about the Internet is that it can't be stopped. Once someone says something about you, it's in the world's hands. I was feeling helpless and scared.

This is how it works with the thirty-two contestants. There are four groups of eight, and each group is given one week to prepare, and your audition is taped for the actual television show. One night we performed our songs, and on the next night the result show would tell who was being voted off the show. Diana DeGarmo and I were the only two who were voted on to the next round that would have twelve people competing in the weekly TV show. The other six in our group went home. Diana and I went home too, but we knew we were coming back. Each of us went home with our own production assistant who spent the next week interviewing family and friends back home and doing sort of life stories on us.

The production assistant who was assigned to me filmed me most of the hours of the days that he was there. He filmed me at home with my friends, family, and daughter. He filmed me eating and brushing my teeth. He talked to my grandmother and wanted to see old photo albums. He asked my friends from the neighborhood about me. At the time, it was a little too much. I couldn't understand why they needed this stuff for a singin' show.

My producer was a white guy who didn't know nothin' about church. He was a little nervous when I told him that we were going to spend a whole day at church. I'm sure that he thought that it would be boring and not something that he would know anything about, but he was surprised. He said after the three-hour service, "I couldn't get enough." God touches everyone, doesn't He?

Before the films of my "life story" had even been processed, it seemed there were articles about me and footage of everything, showing me at church, me with my grandmother, and, most of all, me with Zion. It seemed like out of all the things that were happening with the competition and all the others in the Top 12 who were going home to be filmed, me and my baby were the talk of the Internet. Suddenly, everyone got bold with their thoughts about me havin' a baby and it was all over the chat rooms. People were writing in and complaining that I should not be an icon for American children, because I had sex before I was married and I had a child. They said that my havin' a baby made me a poor example of a young American. I remember someone saying to me, "You should hide your baby. If anyone asks you about it, just say that you don't know what they're talking about." I said, "I can't do that and I won't do that." People on the Internet were writing, "Fantasia is not an American Idol. She is a single mother—that is not a good example for our kids." The producers said, "The choice is up to you."

I put it in God's hands.

Every type of entertainment media was debating my worthiness to be the American Idol. I couldn't believe that so many people were so upset about my baby. It seemed a little hypocritical. I thought that *American Idol* was supposed to represent America, and I knew that there were plenty of baby mamas in America! It hurt me deeply that so many people thought that I was unworthy. They didn't even care about how I sang.

I was overwhelmed and feeling like I had no more words to excuse myself or defend myself. I was keeping the faith but knew that at any time I could be voted off the show.

When the press got close enough to ask me about it, I was constantly open and honest with my responses. I told them being a young mother is not a new thing. I also said to the ones who were sayin' negative things about me that they should have been looking at what I was trying to do *now* instead of focusing on my past.

I was not sure that those answers wouldn't hurt my chances in the competition, but I knew that they were true and that truth was all I had to work with. I had to think about all the things my grandmother had said about truth and honesty. I knew I couldn't lie about Zion and I couldn't pretend that my past hadn't happened. I blamed myself for putting myself into this situation. I was just humbled and scared. I was just waiting for the day for it all to be over.

Behind the scenes, I prayed every day that I could win. I knew that my experience and my love for music had to be more than all those other people. I had been singing since I was five. I had been singin' when everybody else was still playing with blocks. I thought that my situation might keep me from winning, but the Lord knew that I wanted to win. I had asked Him for this opportunity and told Him if I got it, I would change my life. I knew that God wanted me to change my life, so I kept praying that he would possibly open the door one more step for me to win. Sometimes it felt like everyone was against me. Although I still knew in the back of my mind that the media and the industry were already trying to take me out of the race, I wouldn't let 'em take me out that easily. I called and prayed with my mother and grandmother every day. My grandmother was a "prayer warrior," and she had created a "prayer band" at the church. People from everywhere were prayin' for me to win this thing. During the taping days, celebrities would come and meet us. Denzel Washington's wife, Pauletta, who is Christian, came backstage one day and laid hands on me. She said to me, "I love you. I'm praying for you." People everywhere were saying that they were praying for me.

Slowly the bad press started turning into good press and people began to admire me for standing up for myself and my baby and for wanting to create a better life for us. Some people even became supportive and began to write things like "You can't deny her gift." Or "That girl is from the church, so you know she can't be all bad!" Some people started saying that they had a similar experience: "I too had a baby when I was young. Fantasia is doin' her thang and I think it is great!" Some people even wrote things like "I'm a baby mama and Fantasia is my hero!"

God can do so many things you never knew He could do. God and the prayers from all around the world took the pressure off the situation. I felt at peace, no matter what was going to happen.

I dedicated one of my last songs to Zion. It was Barbra Streisand's "What Are You Doing The Rest of Your Life?" It went over as well as "Summertime" had the previous week. People were crying. That song did it for the people. I went out on stage with no shoes on. I wanted to go out and sing that song like it had never been sung before. Ryan Seacrest, the show's host, asked me after the song, "Why are you crying?" I said, with tears in my eyes, "I felt my song." The people were amazed at how raw my emotions were, and how real.

By standing on that stage, I was representing all those women who were single mothers and awesome women. The tide had turned. People were lovin' 'Tasia again.

Even famous people had been givin' me love. It just couldn't get any better than R&B diva Toni Braxton, who actually sent me a Tiffany candle; Denzel and Pauletta Washington, who sent a basket full of body products to me and a gift for Zion; and Kelly Rowland from Destiny's Child who called backstage to speak to me and wish me luck. Like I said, all I ever wanted from this competition was for one person to hear me sing. My prayers had been answered.

In the final group of twelve, we were all going through our own personal transformations from being regular people to having people recognize us everywhere we went and wanting our autographs. Suddenly my days looked different. We were in Hollywood constantly until the end of the show.

The days were grueling at that point. There were fewer people, but the heat was on and the spirit of competition was in the air. We felt the pressure. I had to be somewhere every minute and everyone knew who I was. I was worried about my appearance all the time. I wasn't used to havin' to look cute all the time. I was getting tired and anxious for it to be over. I didn't have any idea that it was just beginning. My producer was always yellin', "Keep it movin', we have places to be!" Every day I would look at myself in the mirror and pinch myself, not believing that I had made it this far and realizing that whatever happened I would never be the same again. I had learned so much and really felt that I had a chance at life. I made it to all of my rehearsals and I was proud of myself for that. I had stood out and made it to the real part of the competition, the part where all of America would be tuning in every week to cheer us on and talk about how we sang. I had made an impression on famous people. It couldn't get any better than this. My life had reached a turning point. I had a real chance to make something of my life. Already my head was spinning about how I would be able to use this experience to finish my GED and how I could sing and make more at the churches and all the different directions that I could actually take just because I had been a part of *American Idol*. And I realized that I could make a good livin' doing what I loved to do best—sing!

The last night of the season, it was down to Diana De-Garmo and me. It had been a fantastic season; some say the best *American Idol* to date. There were so many good singers.

So many of them were really talented. I told myself once again that the fact that I had made it this far was a miracle. I reminded myself that I couldn't possibly win, because of who I was—a single mother and high-school dropout. I didn't want to be disappointed, so I focused on how far I had come instead of what would happen if I won. I thought that America had been generous enough to vote me this far. I thanked God in advance for letting me have this opportunity. I regretted that it might be impossible for me to win, but I had made peace with what the decision was going to be.

Ryan Seacrest came to the stage to announce the winner. He said a few words about the season, and his lips were moving but I couldn't understand a word he was sayin'. I opened my eyes a little bit at a time, thinking that Diana DeGarmo would be on the screen. Instead I looked up to see 'Tasia. Ryan Seacrest was saying *my* name: "The American Idol for 2004 is Fantasia Barrino!" I couldn't believe it. All I had wanted was for one person to hear me sing, and 65 million people heard me and voted for me to be the 2004 American Idol. That was more votes than George W. Bush got. God was standing on that stage. He had been for months. He had been in Georgia with me for both of those auditions. He had brought me to Hollywood and got me through that grueling time, He had got me to the Top 12 and to the Top 2. Being the winner was nothing that I expected. I didn't know how to feel about it but to cry and praise God. He had answered the prayers. My tears poured from my eyes. God's hand was upon me. Emotions were flooding within me. I felt shaky and buckled under my knees. The heel of my new shoe broke, but I didn't even realize it at first. When Ryan Seacrest broke through my dazed wall of emotions and tears, he said, "Why are you crying?" and all I could say was, "I done broke my heel!" Everyone laughed. The 2004 American Idol was still just like y'all.

As the winner of the *American Idol* competition, I was awarded a Ford Focus and a record deal that *could* be worth a million dollars. The record deal was with 19 Recordings and Clive Davis on his new label, J Records. It was overwhelming, considering where I came from. I still didn't know how to react or how to act. I still didn't believe it.

The record deal at J Records seemed like some kind of dream that I would be livin' in. Clive Davis is the man who discovered some of the most unique and unforgettable voices in music: Whitney Houston, Toni Braxton, Alicia Keys, Carlos Santana, and Bruce Springsteen. Was he the one person that God wanted to hear me?

The fact that Clive Davis heard me, met me, and wanted to work with me was beyond belief. I had met Mr. Davis once before in the Top 3 competition. He had been one of the guest judges for this round. He came backstage before the performance and met the three final contestants. He shook hands with Diana DeGarmo and Jasmine Trias and then he came over to me. I expected him to shake my hand as he did the others. Instead, he looked at me and said, "I want you to go out there and sing like you ain't never sang before." I said, startled, "Yes, sir." He left me in shock. I went out and did what he asked me to do, and he had the biggest smile on his face the whole time I was singing. I felt so comfortable and confident that I went right to where the judges were sitting and started singing to him. Clive Davis was singin' with me and dancin'. He was feelin' it.

After I won the following week, I was called to a meeting with Mr. Davis in his J Records office in New York. Mr. Davis's assistant had called and said that he wanted me to come in. I was very nervous. What do you say to an awesome music man? What was I gonna say to someone who is so powerful, mysterious, and invincible? I worried. I decided to just be cool and be *me*. I wouldn't even have known how to pretend to be a different way.

Clive Davis was sitting in a huge brown leather chair. He seemed slumped down, because the chair was so tall. Mr. Davis was twiddling his fingers. When I walked into his beautiful office, he stood up, walked away from the chair, and gave me a kiss. I could smell his cologne and that reminded me of my daddy. Mr. Davis was a groomed man. He walked me around his office, pointing to all the photographs of people he had worked with: Aretha, Whitney, Alicia. I had a smile on my face. He motioned for me to sit down across from him. He had returned to the too-big-for-him chair. He started the conversation by saying, "I want you to tell me, what kind of music do you want to do?" I said, "I am down for doin' anything, but I just want it to be real. I want to make ugly faces when I'm singin' my songs. I just want to be me."

Mr. Davis started playing me some beats, and I was impressed with how *hot* the beats were. Clive is *on it*, I thought to myself. He asked me, "How do you like those beats?" I said jokingly, "You are gangsta!" The whole room became quiet, no one knowing how Mr. Davis would receive such a remark from someone like me. It was dead quiet. Then Mr. Davis started laughing and said to everyone in the room, "Did you hear that, she called me gangsta!" He thought it was really funny. I was slightly embarrassed that I said it like that, but that was what was going through my mind and it was the realest thought that I had at that moment.

The meeting was a success, and all of my nervousness was a thing of the past. I came away from that meeting thinkin', "*Clive Davis knows what he's talking about. He has put a lot of people on the map. I respect him. He's a wise man.*"

When I went on *American Idol*, I wasn't tryin' to win. Besides, it's a pop show and I'm a *soul* singer. My dream was that one day I would perform in front of thousands of people and I did that. I used to say that all I wanted from *Idol* was to get one person to hear me and hook me up. It's all happening because of God's grace. That's the only way to explain it.

MY MOMENT OF
FAITH: WHAT I LEARNED

For by grace are ye saved through faith; and that not of yourselves: it is the gift of God.

EPHESIANS 2:8

- Whatever you put your mind to, you can do. When you have faith you are not supposed to worry.
- When people criticize you, just keep growing and growing regardless of what they say.
- You can do anything you want to.
- Since they said I couldn't, *I did.*

5. Keep Your Head Up

"You aren't ugly, Fantasia" is what I tried to tell myself and what I felt God was saying to me deep down in my heart. But I had a hard time listenin' to Him. Again, I wasn't lettin' Him in, which is the reason why I was walking around with my head hung down.

When I was younger, I didn't listen to my inner voice. I just felt so bad about myself that I couldn't really hear anything that wasn't negative, so God's message of encouragement and love were not getting through. I spent most of my life believin' I was ugly. I would look in the mirror and see my big ole' lips, my dark skin, and how skinny I was and that made me miserable most of the time.

To be honest, I have always had low self-esteem. I would look at my flat chest and compare myself to all the other girls and I would kick my clothes across the floor out of my frustration. The frustration inside me felt like something that was going to rupture and make me bust my gut or somethin'. It was a feeling that just wouldn't go away. I was able to fight this nagging sensation that felt like a pit at the bottom of my stomach when I was with my family or watching TV or singing a song to Zion. Whenever I was with Zion, I always felt like it was all OK. That was the rare time that I was able to keep my head up. Being with Zion let me forget all of my worries and problems. The fact that I never felt like I had enough to give her disappeared when I could see that being with her was what she needed the most. When you are a mother you have an unusual sense of lifelong love that no other relationship can ever beat. Zion looks at me with child's love, which never ever changes. It is the same way I look at her with mommy's love. Zion is always a beautiful sight for my tired eyes. She never looks bad to me. When she is crying or sick or swollen or poutin', she is always beautiful. I feel her looking at me with that same admiration and life-or-death love. Every child thinks that their mommy is beautiful, even if their mommy is *me.*

I remember those moments when Zion was asleep and I was alone with myself with nothin' to do. I remember how bad it felt to have this face and these lips and know that they weren't going anywhere and that I was stuck with them for the rest of my life. These are the times that I hated myself. I didn't know how I was going to get through this life lookin' the way I did. When I was in eighth grade, I used to sit in class watching all the pretty girls and not listening to one word that the teacher was saying. I envied those girls because they always got whatever they wanted, or so it seemed. I envied those that light skin and long wavy hair were requirements for happiness and success. There were other pretty girls who didn't have long hair or light skin in my class, but they had light brown skin like the color of dark coffee with just a little bit of milk thrown in. These girls had pretty perfect white smiles and the brown eyes of angels with long eyelashes. They were pretty girls too, and they *still* didn't look anything like me. I watched the way they moved and the way they picked up their books from their desks and the way they held their books in their arms. I watched the way they picked up their sandwiches and the way they took a bite without getting mayonnaise all over their lips. I memorized the sight of those girls, hoping to become one of them.

What was so frustrating about all of this was that I couldn't understand why I looked the way that I did. I looked at Mama with child's love. My mama was beautiful to me. And you *know*, I loved my daddy and thought he was the most handsome man in the world. How could Mama and Daddy have made such an ugly girl like me? I wondered. The confusion would bring tears to my eyes. Sometimes my teacher would catch me in my daydream and ask, "Fantasia, why are you crying?" And I would say, "No reason, ma'am, I'm just thinkin' about some things." And the teacher would say, "You should be thinkin' about the test tomorrow." Then she would say, "Fantasia, open your book to page forty-two, please. We are on the third paragraph." This embarrassment of being behind in class would give 'em something more to tease me about. It was yet another misunderstanding. I was thinking about something that was important to me and everyone else just thought I was dumb.

My mind wandered right back to the pretty girls who always had boyfriends. The pretty girls always got what they wanted from their parents. The pretty girls were smarter and richer and got better grades. With this face and these lips, I thought, I was just always going to be on the outside, lookin' in.

There was a lot of drama at my house when I was twelve years old. Truth is, I had a lot to learn. My mother used to suffer through those nights when I went to her cryin' and screamin' about my looks. I told her that I hated myself. "I got big lips, I'm too skinny, and it makes it hard for me! I can't take it!" I used to say. I was giving her an awful time. Mama didn't know what to do with me. I could hear her praying for me at night when she thought I was asleep. She would come into my room and pray over my sleeping head.

My mother would always tell me that I was as pretty as any other girl. When I would complain, she would say, "Fantasia, don't worry about it." I would say, "But I'm skinny!" And she would say, "Don't worry about it! God made you skinny so you could move through life easier." I would say, "I hate my lips!" And she would say, "Don't worry about it! God gave you those lips so that you could sing better." I would say, "I have no chest!" She would say, "Don't worry

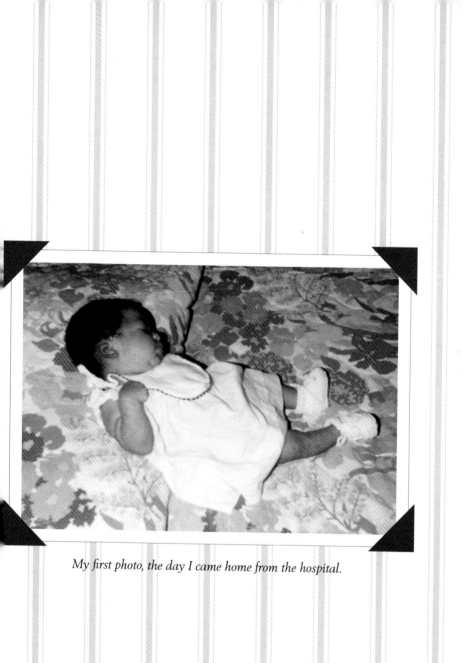

My first photo, the day I came home from the hospital.

My first musical instrument—my rattle!

*I had some spunk
even when I was two.*

The "famous" Barrino Family.

My first real bling.

Makin' it big in High Point,
North Carolina,
the Furniture Capital
of the World.

The house where it all happened, 511 Montlieu Avenue.

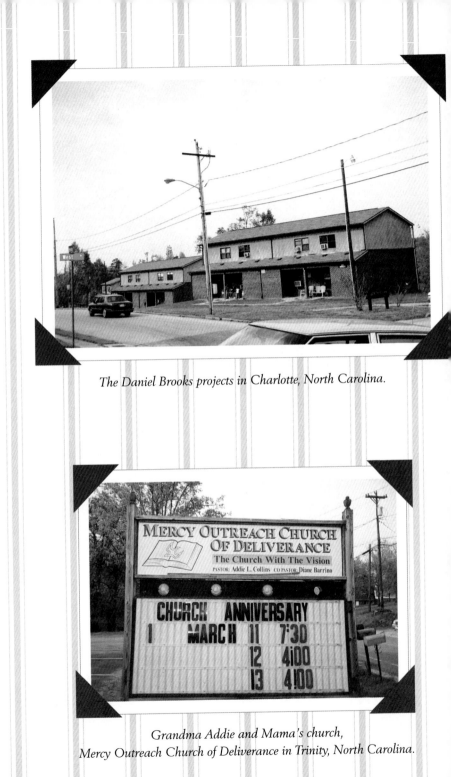

The Daniel Brooks projects in Charlotte, North Carolina.

Grandma Addie and Mama's church,
Mercy Outreach Church of Deliverance in Trinity, North Carolina.

A proud baby mama.

The man who showed me respect, J.B.

about it, God gave you a little chest, but he gave you big lungs and a big gift. He couldn't give you everything so he gave you what you could use."

As difficult as those moments were with my mother, what she was tellin' me started to sink in. I realized that there were things that I couldn't change about myself and there were things that I could do something about. My mother told me to take the qualities that I had and work with them. She used to always quote this famous prayer: "God grant me the serenity to accept the things that I cannot change, the courage to change the things I can, and the wisdom to know the difference."

I decided I was going to stop complainin' about the things I couldn't change and just "work it," like Mama used to say. So, when I was about twelve or thirteen I became a girl who was into fashion and hair. I wore all kinds of crazy outfits and my mother let me do it. Blue fingernail polish, food coloring in my hair, ripped T-shirts. Anything that said I was "in da house." I did all kinds of things to my hair: it was slicked down, standing on end, braided on the sides—anything just to stand out and let people know that 'Tasia was as good as those pretty girls.

I looked at magazines all the time. The magazines were filled with models and pretty girls, and I looked at them every time I could get my hands on one. I would get them from the garbage or if they were left on a seat at the doctor's office or, once in a while, Mama would even buy me one. I never was able to read the articles, but I was only interested in how everyone *looked*. I would stand in the mirror and pose like them and try to smile like them and hold my head the way they did. I somehow thought that if I read those magazines enough, somehow I would start looking like some of them.

My mother tells a story about the day I was in the eighth grade and went to school in one of my self-made outfits. It was a denim shirt tied up around my belly button with rips torn into the sleeves and back. I also had a denim miniskirt that I had redesigned by cutting the bottom off the skirt and then taking what little was left and cutting the fabric on a diagonal so it ended right below my panty line. When I came into our yellow kitchen on Montlieu Avenue that morning in my outfit, my mother was shocked. Her mouth just hung open. She couldn't get any words out. She knew how sensitive I was about my appearance, so she didn't say what she wanted to say and let me go to school like that. Mama knew what would happen. So I went to school in my "hot to trot" denim outfit, fishnet stockings, and stack-heeled shoes. When I returned home that afternoon a little earlier than usual, my mother saw that I had tied someone else's jacket around my waist, covering all that needed to be hidden. My mother laughed to herself and asked, "Fantasia, why are you wearing that shirt around your waist?" Humbly, I said, "All the kids at school laughed at me and told me to cover up!" My mother had known, but she wanted me to learn for myself when being "too cute" wasn't "cute."

That evening after dinner, Mama came into my room to talk to me about what happened at school that day. I cried to her, telling her that I thought my outfit was like the clothes that I saw in the magazines. I told her that it hurt me that the girls and guys were laughing about my ripped T-shirt and my skirt that was too short and the hem was crooked. I pleaded with Mama to tell me what had gone wrong, because I didn't understand. Everyone knew that I was different and liked looking unusual like the models.

Mama explained to me that that my outfit was trying too hard to be something that I wasn't. She said that what everyone could see in that outfit was fakeness. She said, "Everyone knows you 'Tasia. They all grew up with you. They know you are not like them clothes. They know you are not those rips and tears. They know that you are a girl who loves the Lord and who is anointed. They know that the Holy Spirit is in you. That is why they were laughing, because you were being something that you are not. You were being a *fake*."

I asked Mama, "How can I fix it?" And she said, "Fantasia, the thing that my mama always told me was to keep my head up." I asked Mama what that meant, and she said, "It means to be proud of who you are and what you are. If you are a child of God, don't act like you are a child of Satan. Keep your head up and be proud of who you are and what you came from, no matter if it is good or bad." I listened to what Mama was saying and needed to think about it more. I did remember Grandma Addie saying that sometimes when I was leaving her house. She would kiss me on my forehead and say in my ear, "Keep your head up."

Self-esteem is something that I have struggled with. Just being happy with the way I looked was impossible for me when all the pretty girls looked better than me. That is why I tried so hard to make myself look different with different clothes and wild nail colors and wild shoes. There were no similarities between those pretty girls and me, no matter how hard I tried to look like them. It's taken a long time for my self-esteem to grow stronger. The way that I improved it happened shortly after that talk with Mama. I could feel myself finally growing tired of all the hate inside my heart that was slowly eating away at me. I was looking in the mirror one day, putting on my blue shimmery eye shadow and my red, red lipstick. My hand slipped, and the lipstick went off my lips and smeared above my lip. Instead of wiping it right away, I stood there and looked at my face for five solid minutes. I looked like a clown. My stomach was churning and tears were running down my face. I felt sick to my stomach because what was at the pit of my stomach was self-hate. I remember thinking to myself that I had to change my insides because putting all this stuff all over my face was not making me prettier. It was making me a clown. I wanted finally to lift my head.

I thought to myself, What if I loved myself instead of hating myself? I realized that I needed to have a real relationship with myself first and not worry so much about my relationships with my girlfriends and B. and the other boys. Instead of the kids at school making me feel ugly with their mean nicknames and constant teasing, I needed to come up with some names for myself that were better than their names. Instead of B. making me feel ugly with his disrespect and neglect, I learned that I had to drown out his voice and make my own voice the loudest. Instead of the girls calling me "Big Lips" and "Snaggle Tooth" I told myself that I was "Beautiful Lips" and "Pretty Smile." I started talkin' to myself. Instead of the teachers making me feel dumb, I had to tell myself that I was smart. I decided that the "I am so ugly" song had to go. It didn't really matter to the outside world what song I sang to *myself*, so I decided to change my song from "I am ugly" to "I am beautiful." Instead of walking around with my head hung down low, I decided to stand up straight, lift my head, and have some pride in myself. Although it was hard at first, because I wasn't really convinced, I started look- ing in the mirror more instead of avoiding it. I started going over my face one feature at a time and saying to myself, "My eyebrows look good." "My nose is good." Like Mama said, "My lips are good because they are better to sing with." "My crooked teeth can be fixed." I looked at my short hair and imagined it in red or blond. I imagined it in a ponytail or in braids. I said, "I can make it anything I want. I can control this." Since that day, eight years ago, I am still always prancin' around and my head is always up, and I finally look like I own *myself.* I look in the mirror and I say, "This is me, and I am the bomb!"

I know, you think 'Tasia's trippin' again, but I'm really not. It is just that this is the only way for me to see myself. And the only way for you to see yourself, too. I don't want to go "Hollywood." I don't want to change myself. I don't want to change God's perfect plan. I don't want to think that change comes with money. I wanted to change my look with a new attitude and that's all I needed. If I didn't change my own view of myself, no one else could.

Feeling better about yourself also means changing your actions. I finally got sick of hearin' the negative things about my skinniness. The boys used to call me S&B, which was short for "Skin and Bones." The first part of changing from a weakling to a strong woman was *to stop bein' and actin' weak*. I had to stop letting people tell me who I was when I knew me best. I had to stop being so *sensitive*.

Just like everyone else, I want to keep my body in shape. Whenever I'm on the road, I go to the hotel's gym and do the treadmill for as long as I can. It's not easy, though, because I don't have a set work schedule, so it's hard to have a set exercise schedule. When I get off the road and go back home to North Carolina, Mama always makes sure that I can eat some of my favorite foods, like fried chicken, sweet potatoes, Mama's beef stew, and chicken Alfredo with broccoli, because she feels like I deserve it after months on the road and eating restaurant food. My favorite foods are not the healthiest foods in the world, but they sure taste good! When I struggle with the guilt of eating the foods that I love and that I miss so much, I realize that Fantasia is not her imperfections. I love myself, even if I'm not skinny or perfect. I am happy—finally. With God in my life, I always see that I am beautiful—even when others don't.

I even love my lips now. Once I began to love my lips,

everyone else did too. I have heard about women who pay thousands of dollars for those injections to make their lips look more like mine. I was blessed with lips like this and I don't have to pay a dime for them! All those years, I was afraid of what guys would think about my lips. Now, I have guys come up to me and say, "You have beautiful lips. Can I kiss them?" The answer is always, "No!" of course, but what a difference those comments have made for my self-esteem. I have to beat the boys off of me because of my lips. This is how God made me. That was his plan for me to finally see that His gifts are not always punishments.

Having positive self-esteem does take time. Like I say, it's a lifelong process. I think most women go through it. First, we're dissatisfied with ourselves, then we start complainin' about body parts and start tryin' to hide them. Then we make our peace with them and start learning how to use them. Now, when I sign autographs, I draw the image of my lips under my signature. My lips are my autograph. Instead of trying to think of a positive message to tell other young women, my lips say it all. They are my trademark. That is why I had the image of my lips tattooed on my hip, so I never forget what made me who I am today. These are my big lips that God gave me to sing with.

After *Idol*, I started seeing myself in pictures regularly, and I noticed my skin looked a half a shade lighter than before and much brighter. My skin really wasn't lighter, of course, but happiness and confidence had put a glow on my face. Even though my face did look different from old family photographs because I had a professional makeup artist sometimes, I know it was also because I was glowing *inside*, and not only did I look different, I felt different. I even used to hate my smile because it was so wide. In all of my earlier photos, I didn't smile very much. But now, I smile so wide that I can brighten up a whole room. That's what people say, and I finally believe them.

It may seem hard to believe, but I also used to hate my name. Fantasia was such an unusual name and nobody else had it except for that stupid movie. Since I was already feeling like an outsider because of my looks, the name was just another thing for people to tease me about. The movie, *Fantasia*, had come out, and the kids were teasing me at school sayin', "I saw your movie and I didn't like it!" I hadn't seen the movie and didn't know anything about it. Just thinking about it, I fantasized that the movie would be about a girl named Fantasia and she would be just like me, *and* she was happy. My mother bought a bootleg copy of the movie for me to see and she says that all she could hear from the other room after I put it on was me cryin' and sayin,' "This movie ain't nothin'. This ain't nothin'!" Turns out the movie was about magic and magic potions. I was mostly disappointed because the happiness in the movie wasn't the happiness that I needed to believe in. It was a cartoon. There wasn't even a girl named Fantasia in the movie. *And Fantasia wasn't real.* Now when I think about the name Fantasia, it sounds unusual, like a singer's name. Grandma Addie was right when she picked this name for me. It sounds like "Aretha" or "Stevie Wonder" or "Elton John." It's different and that's what makes it memorable.

In case you're wondering, I don't need a man to make me feel beautiful, either—my family takes care of that. My grandma never misses one of my TV appearances. After each one, she calls and cries on the phone saying how beautiful I looked on stage. My mother also catches every TV appearance and she always calls or leaves me messages commenting on how I was "rockin" those shoes or "wearin' the heck out of that dress." Zion's opinion matters the most, because I want to be a mother who she can look up to. I want to be a mother who she might hope to become someday. Mama always puts Zion on the phone and she always says without fail, "Mommy, you are so pretty." Why would I need a man to make me feel any better than that?

Like I said, there is no greater relationship than the relationship that we have with our children. Our children are gifts from God, and although it's a struggle to face the consequences of having kids young, we all have to keep our heads up and be proud of our children and not ashamed of them. People have a way of making us baby mamas ashamed of our kids and our circumstances, but the thing about our kids is that they are totally pure and innocent and they can be anything we want them to be or anything they want to be.

For me, I think of Zion as the princess and strong woman that I want to be an example of. Mainly I want her to not become the person that her father is. Because I treat Zion like what I want for her, she falls into it. So, baby mamas, don't do that to your kids—treating them like you wish you could treat their fathers. Even if they do look just like their daddy, or even if they act a little like him, your kids are not their fathers. They are precious gifts from God and they deserve a future of love and happiness and *hope*. Cherish the relationship with your children; it's the only lifelong relationship you will have, and it's the most important relationship.

The love that comes from your children is the *truth*. It doesn't depend on how you look or how your dress fits you. When your children look at you, it is almost as if they are blind to any of the outside things that the world is so concerned with. They can't see your clothes or your makeup or that you need to get your hair done. All they see is *you. Don't get me cryin'!*

Of course I would love to someday have a man who makes me feel beautiful. I have tried having a relationship during this year of *Idol*, and it hasn't always worked out. Dealing with men can be hard work! I have dated several young men who have become friends, mostly, but one relationship in particular could have become something, but we were both too young and too immature to handle it. Although it hurts me to think of losing him, I have already put my romantic life back into God's hands. Although I have been able to build my self-esteem substantially, sometimes I have moments that are filled with loneliness. No matter how confident I have become and no matter how much my family and friends support me, it's only natural that people want to be paired up. I think it hurts the most for us single mothers because we had a child *with* someone and now something is missing, no one is there. As all women, I do want a man in my life to help me raise my child, but I'm at least ready and willing to wait for the right one.

The rest of my self-esteem story ends much like a fairy tale. When I was shooting *Idol* and I had made it to the Top 4, my friend Erin and I were walking through the mall in Los Angeles looking for the MAC store. I had started wearing MAC makeup during the *Idol* competition because they gave it to all of the contestants. We were looking for the store and I was pretending that I was one of the people on the displays over the makeup counter. I was making faces, poutin' my lips out, and pretending that I had a deal with MAC to endorse the lipsticks. Erin said, "Wouldn't it be funny if MAC offered you some kind of endorsement deal because of your lips?" I said, "That is *never* going to happen."

About two months later, I got a call from someone from my management company saying that MAC called and they wanted to use me for a line of Fantasia lipsticks. The lipstick would be called the Fantabulous line. They proposed creating two different shades of Lip Glass for me. The two were to be called Fantabulous 1 and Fantabulous 2. Lip Glass is really just lip gloss. I couldn't believe it. I couldn't stop shaking. It was unbelievable that a cosmetic company would want to use me and promote a woman who looks like me. I loved the colors and they never ran or smudged off my big lips. I had a blast working with the folks at MAC and picking out the colors for my two Fantabulous shades. We decided on one that was a deep purple and another that was a shiny bronze color.

Soon after that, I was also asked to endorse American Rag jeans—can you believe it? S&B, Skin and Bones, endorsing a line of jeans. It seems like the person that I told myself I was, I *wasn't*. The people at MAC and American Rag saw me as "beautiful," "appealing," and "real." It makes me wonder why I wasted so much time hating myself when it was true that people did love me and who I was. The thing that I learned is that loving yourself is the only way to live.

The American Rag was perfect for me because they are the only jeans that are cut for women who have especially long legs. I have always been all legs. I was told they wanted me because they had seen my body type and liked my style and what I stood for. The ads had a picture of me in the jeans and it reads, "I'm an American." They thought that I represented the casual side of being an American and an *American Idol*. They said that I am *real*. American Rag even designed a line of jeans with the outline of my lips on the pocket in silver studs. Isn't that a trip?

During my American Rag endorsement, I was also asked to be a part of the Macy's Thanksgiving Day Parade. They asked me to be on the United States Postal Service float, which was the Winner's Float, alongside Olympic track stars. I was asked to sing "I Believe," which was fitting for me because although I had dreams, I still couldn't believe that I was standing on that float in New York City, in the most famous parade in the *world*. Who would have believed that I, an ugly ducklin' with a strange name, would became an American Idol and a model? But if you believe in God, everything is possible.

What is *impossible* is going through life feeling that you have no worth. We girls all have to stop believing the media and the images that they keep puttin' out there for us and our daughters that make us hate ourselves and make us feel like we are not beautiful and not good enough, when we really are. Most people are sick of seeing tall, skinny girls with perfect faces and perfect features. These women and men don't really represent the majority of the population, who are trying everything including surgery, takin' pills, exercising themselves to death, and starving themselves just in hopes of looking like them, with no luck.

Being beautiful is a state of mind. It has nothing to do with your physical self. Think of all those stories that we hear about people like Oprah Winfrey, who was told that she could never be on television because her face wasn't pretty enough. Now she owns television with the biggest talk show ever and is a TV and film actress as well.

You never know what you are capable of until you decide what you want and then you just have to go for it. By just being on *American Idol*, I have been blessed with so many other opportunities. Again, I think it was because I finally found my gift. If you have something that you want to do or become, find the people who have the same passion that you have. Go to the places they hang out and let them know you're there. Show them you have a gift and that you can contribute to the group. Show them you believe in yourself and that you are eager to listen and learn. You can do anything that you put your mind to. Think about me and where I've come from. Remember, all the things I've been through and all the people who have doubted me and all the times I doubted myself. And one last thing I need you to remember: Always keep your head up.

MY MOMENT OF
FAITH: WHAT I LEARNED

Trust in the Lord with all thine heart; and lean not unto thine own understanding. In all thy ways acknowledge Him, and He shall direct thy paths.

PROVERBS 3:5–6

Make yourself feel pretty:

- Buy yourself lingerie and wear it when you're alone. You can make yourself feel pretty.
- Tell yourself that you are beautiful. And mean it. Even if you are not all the way there.
- Keep a nice tight stomach.
- Put effort into your appearance, if only to impress yourself.

Give God thanks ahead of time:

- I never say I don't deserve the things that have happened to me. It sometimes still wows me, but I knew that God had great things in store for me. I just thank Him for these things that blow my mind. I know that I have to stay in His will.

6. Give
Props Where Props
Are Due

God **wants** all of His children to keep their heads up. That is why God gave all of His children talents and wants each of us to acknowledge each other and our God-given talents. God wants us to all give and get our props! I am a child of God, so in my spirit there should be no jealousy, competitiveness, or playa' hatin'. You will hear people say that I have a "big heart." You will also hear people say that I am "generous to a fault." I believe that there is no such thing as that. How can there be fault in being generous? I do consider myself to be generous, but not to a fault. It is in my blood to want to help people and to love them.

This is not to say that I have always been like that. As you know, I'm not perfect. And back in the days when I was envying all the other girls who were prettier than me and had more money than me and more things than me, I did feel *jealous* of them. I ain't gonna lie. But when I think back to those days and those feelings, I realize that feelin' jealous or hatin' on people for what they had didn't bring me to where I am today. And those feelings were one of the things that kept me from improving my life.

My mother used to say, "What goes around, comes around." When I was younger, I didn't really understand the truth in that. Now I see that she meant you can either send out negative energy, like jealousy, gettin' that in return, or you can send out praise and receive that back instead. The energy that I spent on wishing I could be someone else or having what they had was a total waste of my time and energy, which I could have spent growing as a person and improving myself. Instead of sitting in that classroom daydreaming about those other girls, I wish I had been propping them up and complimenting their hair or saying how pretty their faces were. It would have brought me much closer to what I thought I wanted without creating those feelings of tension and pity that was my whole school experience. I wish I had known then what I know now about how to be real with people and how to give props when props are due.

I guess I have learned about props from the church. Holiness makes you vocal. It lets you say what you feel. Sometimes, instead of saying "Hallelujah" when I heard a beautifully sung riff, I would turn to whomever was standing near me and ask: "Did you hear that?" At church I was exposed to a whole lot of singers. Most of those singers had big talent. They were not only singin', they could *saang*! Church singers typically listen to a lot of different styles of music, and every style influences them. Within gospel there are hymns, stomps, choral pieces, solos, contemporary, traditional, and now even hip-hop. Gospel music is truly special because the gospel artists find so many ways to express their love and appreciation for Jesus. Gospel singers have the gift to be able to put the passion of loving God into their music in a way that touches people who don't even believe in God. These singers are able to show their love for God in a romantic way that musically feels like rhythm and blues, which touches everybody's heart. Certain emotions in gospel music need to borrow from other styles. Certain phrases about loving Jesus can be scatted and not traditionally sung. The unusual approach makes the song stand out as well as that particular lyric. It is all in the delivery. Sometimes an old-time hymn may be updated to borrow influences from blues music. What I have always loved about gospel music is that it takes from the black experience, and so the music has a feeling that touches everyone who has ever known about pain and struggle, even if you are not saved. The amazing thing that gospel music does is touch people's spirits with all the truth, drama, and emotion that come from livin'.

By being in church, I saw how important people are to me. When you're in the church you get a chance to see people going through every period of their lives. At church you see how fragile people can be. You see people who are happy and thanking God for blessings, but you also see people who have just lost their child or husband or have been diagnosed with a deadly disease. You see the most faithful people angry and questioning God's love. Other times, you see people who are wantin' one more chance and they are worshipping Him so strongly that you can taste their desperation. Church folks have taught me everything I know about life and happiness and sorrow, good and evil, riches and poverty. This has given me a loving view of people and that is why, to this day, I never meet a stranger. I have a loving attitude about everyone who I meet. I guess that is what makes me "country." I'm willing to be open with the way that I feel about people. I have no strain about lovin' people.

When I won *American Idol*, besides making my album, my first experience was going on the *American Idol* tour. The Top 10 Idols performed in fifty-two cities, showcasing our talent. The press spoke so much about how generous I was with the spotlight on the tour. I never understood how I could have been any other way.

The tour began in mid-July and ended in early October in Singapore. We went to fifty-two cities. Our normal schedule was to perform one night, then travel and have the next night off. We went to fifty-two cities in North America and then went to Singapore, which was a first for the tour. We visited Salt Lake City, Utah; Milwaukee, Wisconsin; Cincinnati, Ohio; Sunrise, Florida; Toronto, Ontario; and Honolulu, Hawaii, just to name a few. It was an awesome chance to see America and meet the people who put us where we were.

We rehearsed for two weeks in Los Angeles before the

tour started. The rehearsals were hard, but it was fun for me to be back with my other favorite Idols like Jasmine, Camille, La Toya and George, remembering and reliving all that had happened in such a short amount of time. Millions of people had watched *American Idol* week after week, and fans became addicted to experiencing the ups and downs of regular people living their dreams. The *American Idol* tour is a way for the audience to see their favorite singers and enjoy watching everyone perform without having to worry about who will get eliminated and end up being crushed at the end of the night.

When the tour rehearsals first started, I naïvely thought the songs had been divided equally among everyone. When I looked at the song list, I had a bunch of songs. They basically had me doing the whole show. I was performing solos and duets and group numbers—it was crazy! So when it was time to go to the first official rehearsal, it seemed that the producers were trying to make it the "Fantasia Show" because I had won. I felt like it wasn't fair because there were nine other winners there and the people didn't only want to see me and Diana DeGarmo. I wanted to share the spotlight, so I gave up a couple of my solos. I wanted everyone to be able to have a chance to sing and be *heard*. We had all worked hard to get there and this was the time that everyone could show what they had. I was known for disrupting rehearsal by changing things around. I would say to the producers, "Let so and so sing that one!" or "Let him sing that, too!" We all love to sing, so I was simply givin' props where they were due. Sharin' the love—givin' everyone their chance to receive the love from our audience.

Everyone in the Top 10 was so likable and so talented. We got along so well. (I know most people don't believe that, but it's true.) Of course, we had our disagreements, much like brothers and sisters do. We argued about what to eat, or who was late getting to the stage, or we teased each other when our hair was not done or when someone was losing or gaining weight. There were small disagreements but because of the amount of stress we were under, the disagreements often escalated into something bigger. Sometimes there was "drama"—but only until show time. One of the producers told me that we were actually the best group ever in terms of gettin' along and lookin' out for each other.

Sometimes, the Idols were sick of seein' each other because we were sick of ourselves. We would see each other in passing and joke, "You haven't gone home yet?" We were getting *tired*. There was not a lot to do when we weren't singing or on the bus. Jasmine, John, and Diana were all traveling with their mothers. Amy Adams was engaged and had her fiancé with her. La Toya was married and was always in her room talking on the phone to her husband. There were not a lot of places to go and not much time, so Camille and I just spent our evenings alone, talking until we couldn't talk any more.

Jennifer Hudson and La Toya London were so supportive and always helped me out when I needed them. For example, I had a dentist appointment and needed an emergency root canal. I asked them to sing my songs and they did. La Toya, Jennifer, and I were all tight, and when I asked them to sing in my place, it was always cool. I felt the same thing about the other talented Idols. Most of the people who are on *Idol* don't just listen to pop radio and R&B radio alone. They listen to all kinds of music and appreciate all of it. They come from all over the country with all kinds of music backgrounds. I'm sure that I taught the singers on our tour some things about gospel music, but I learned a lot from them, too. One of the things I learned from other singers is to be more subtle in my delivery of certain songs. Everything can't be so dramatic and full of hollerin' like church music usually is. I needed to learn that. I learned from some of the other Idols to take my time with a song. I also learned from all of them that your roots are what make up your style as a singer. I found out that what comes natural to me is what usually works best.

I did feel confident about my performance, not because I won on *Idol* or because I thought I was the best, but because I knew that I was very comfortable being me, and to me that is what makes me a good singer. Every night, I felt like I was going out there givin' 'em my type of singin', which is singin' from the church. It's the singin' that I had been doing as long as I could remember. I took every song and was always " 'Tasia wit' it." Sometimes the other singers would try to switch up their styles, but I never switched mine. I kept it 'Tasia. For me, a jazz song or a country song or whatever, I just sang it like I was makin' 'Tasia art. I always want my singin' to be beautiful and I always want it to be a part of me.

The *American Idol* tour was a very busy time for me. After three years of sitting on the couch, I could not have imagined being *sooo* busy. Everyone else got to use their days off relaxin', sightseein', or just kickin' it. I, on the other hand, was busy making my album. Winning American Idol meant that my album had to be completed as soon as possible so that my fans could hear my music. On nights before a scheduled day off, I was taken to the airport immediately following a show to fly to Los Angeles to work on my album. The tour schedule was crazy, and it was often frustrating to live on a bus for almost four months! When I felt frustrated and restless, I would think back to those nights on the porch at Montlieu Avenue, singing like it was all I knew and the only thing we had to call our own. Those nights I was dreamin' that someday I would have the "problem" of being on tour and singing my heart out every day to thousands of people. Every time I remembered that dream, I was just thankful to be on that plane, with no sleep.

I have grown so much in myself, so I am able to say to you, now, in all honesty, that everybody on the tour was *really good*. I could never hate on them, ever. The other Idols were amazed at how excited I was when others were singin' and doin' their thing. If someone hit a great note or did something that moved my spirit, I was sayin' somethin' out loud. I was constantly walking around backstage sayin', "Did you hear that note?"

On tour, my favorite Idols were George Huff, Jennifer Hudson, Camille Velasco, and La Toya London. George Huff is a *baad* brotha' who had very good vocal control on the tour. I don't really recognize notes and I can't read music, but George knows notes and his vocal arrangements were so crazy. He could do things that left me wondering, "How did he do *that?*" George was very soulful and you could tell that he, too, was raised in the church. When George performed he made you want to get up out of your seat. I always see myself as having an old sound and George does too. When he would smile, he would brighten up my whole day.

Jennifer Hudson reminded me of Roberta Flack. Jennifer didn't need a microphone. I was just amazed when I heard her sing and always thought, Where is she comin' from with that voice? Jen had that type of power! You could hear her coming from a mile away. She was just soulful, soulful, soulful!

La Toya was different than the others. She was laid back and soothing with her singin'. Her voice was light but soulful. I could sit back and relax when listening to La Toya's voice. She has a beautiful voice with such good vocal control. Her voice reminds me of all those times when I was growing up and my mother was cleaning the house on Montlieu Avenue and she would have Anita Baker playing.

John Stevens had an older vocal and he sounded like Frank Sinatra, and people love Frank Sinatra. That is what got him to the Top 10. John had a *different* vocal, and when he didn't have a good round on the show, it was just because he was so young and nervous. He would be singing Broadway music and he was sixteen and doing it so well. When you really heard him, you could hear that he had a beautiful voice and it was a little sexy. The older ladies loved him.

Camille is someone I became very close with during my *American Idol* experience. She reminded me of me a little bit and I had that bond with her of going through struggles and overcoming some obstacles. We both fight for what we believe and know that nothing is impossible. We are still close to this day.

All the Idols stood out for me and made me realize that I wished I played the keyboards, so I could do more with my songs and be able to play them as soon as they come to my mind. That just goes back to me thinkin' about how much I have, but how much I lost when I was younger and not going to school. I should know how to read music as much as I love it. It made me sad when I saw George up there, playin' and singin' and writin' his own songs right when they came to his head. What power that would be. If you love music and you're studying music, you'll have the power to create whatever comes into your mind and your spirit. It just reminds me that while I have had this extraordinary change in my life, there is still so much that I have missed that I want to catch up on.

When the tour was over, everyone was tired and eager to get back home. I was the only crybaby, of course. I cried and cried. Those nine other singers had become my family. I learned something from every one of them. Every night, no matter what had happened earlier that day, we all got on the stage and would "work it out!" I can't say enough about how awesome everyone was.

As you can see, I am not competitive anymore, not like I was with the girls when I was in school. Now, I just get inspired by *talent*. Those years of envying other girls really taught me that using that negative energy doesn't work and it doesn't make you grow. The only person that I compete with is 'Tasia. I'm very hard on myself. I love to sing with good singers because of all they can do with their voices. It feels wonderful to hear my voice against theirs or blend with their voices. I'm always taking notes in my head about my performances and about what I have to do better the next time.

I have come a long way from that envious "ugly" little girl that I used to be. But I'm not talking about my looks. What was probably the ugliest thing about me was that I wanted what other people had. To this day, I don't know what happened to all those pretty little girls with boyfriends who I used to envy. I don't know if their baby daddies did the same things that Zion's daddy did to me. I don't know if they have children they are raisin' on their own. Or if they are happily married. I don't know if they are successful or not. Who knows? *People are people.* And everybody has their highs and lows in life. What I do know is that when I cleansed my heart of being envious and jealous and focused on my life and my music and God, the blessings just started pourin' in. Probably the most important thing that I have learned after all I have been through is the simplest thing: Give props where props are due!

The experience that I had with the Idols taught me a lot

about the difference between being *friends* and *being friendly*. What I have learned is that friends are deeper than the people you are friendly with. With friends there are no barriers. With people you are friendly with, although they are friendly to you, that doesn't mean that they sometimes don't have their own interests at heart and their own barriers. The thing about true friends is that they help you to grow and be better people and you do the same for them. Real friends feel like family even though there is no blood relation.

My first real friends *were* family, my cousins, Kima and Kadijah, Aunt Rayda's daughters. Back in those days, we were like the Three Musketeers. We all had other friends, but we were *family*, and we were always in church together because we were always with our mothers. Kima and Kadijah were like my sisters, and our mothers treated us like triplets. We sometimes wore the same clothes, and once we all got the same baby dolls at Christmastime. We were all happy to get our matching baby dolls. One Christmas, mine was the white version of the doll while Kima and Kadijah had the black version. My mom didn't say anything about it, hoping that I hadn't noticed that my baby doll was white. It really hadn't mattered to me, but Aunt Rayda asked my mama over Christmas dinner, "Why didn't you get Fantasia the black doll?" Embarrassed, my mother said, "Because they ran out of the black ones and the white ones were all they had left." In my neighborhood, the white ones were only a last resort. Kima and Kadijah just used to say that my baby was mixed. In my room, there were all types of odd dolls based on when my mother had enough money to get what they had left on the shelf. I had dolls with one leg shorter than the other and dolls with two different shoes. That was when 'Dijah was four, I was five, and Kima was seven. We played house with those babies until they fell apart. I remember those broken-off arms and legs strewn all over my room, reminding me of all those hours of play with my two favorite cousins. It still makes me smile.

Today, Kima, who is twenty-two, has three daughters of her own and is happily married. Kadijah is nineteen and in college. They call me all the time just to check in with me. Although their lives are so different from mine, I know they would do anything for me and I would do anything for them. It's our memory of those broken doll parts that binds us together, forever.

Another person in my life who really keeps me grounded is my brother Rico. He has been a lifesaver and a friend. Even though he is very proud of me for winning *American Idol*, he doesn't take this "fame" thing too seriously. When we're on the road together, everything is a joke with him. We play jokes on each other constantly and we laugh all the time.

Being on the road is the hardest thing I have ever done. I'm constantly losing sleep or having uncomfortable, interrupted sleep. We are traveling on buses, which are nice, but they can leave you feeling cramped, eating fast food, being "on" all day long singin', smilin', and signin' autographs, even when I haven't had enough sleep and all I really want is a little time to myself. Rico and I keep each other laughing to make it all easier.

One time during this past year when I had worked every single day without a break for weeks, I started to feel like I couldn't do it anymore and I needed a break. I felt sick and weak. I felt like giving up. My stomach was upset every morning and I could barely walk straight. Rico saw me gettin' weak and he said to me with the straightest face I have ever seen on him, "I never want to hear you say that you can't do anything." He said, "Think of all we have been through. We thought we would never be here, but we *are*." And he was right.

Although Rico is a joker, he is also a prayin', lovin' man who would do anything for me. He is a character who keeps everybody laughing, especially the limousine drivers and the people who work in the hotels and restaurants. But with all that laughter, he still manages to bring home and prayer with him. Rico reminds me of my mama. Keeping him with me on the road reminds me every day about where I come from and where I will return after the last song is sung.

When it comes to thinking about the other people who have made a difference in my life, I think about some of the girls who showed me what friendship is, although in some cases it was fleeting.

I once had a friend named Tamika. She and I were best friends. We were always hangin' at the Candy Lady's cart. The Candy Lady sold candy, soda pop, pickles, bubble gum, and ice cream. We called ourselves "the Candy Lady

Queens." I loved Tamika because she was funny and bold and always made me want to be as cool as her, in those days. Our friendship ended when we got to middle school, though, and Tamika started hanging around with the really cool girls, the girls who thought they were gangstas. We called them the "hoodie hoodchicks," because they wore sweatshirts with hoods trying to look like the tough boys in the neighborhood. When Tamika started hanging with them, we stopped hanging around each other. I was still into church then and wondered why Tamika's family let Tamika do a lot more than other girls our age could do, like smokin' cigarettes and cursin'. This was around fifth and sixth grade, when I was only eleven years old. I couldn't keep up with Tamika and, although hanging around with the hoodchicks seemed excitin', I knew I could never do those things. I had to let her go. Sometimes I still miss those days going to the Candy Lady with Tamika and eating hard pickles and salty chips.

From when I was fourteen to now, the definition of a friend has changed a lot. When I was fourteen, I would depend on my older friends, like Tonya, to give me a place to stay when I had left my parents' house and needed a place to go. I remember idolizing the girls who were older than me. They had their own apartments and they had no parents around telling them what to do. They made their own rules and that included letting me stay there doing whatever I wanted. Tonya thought she was being my friend and, in some ways, she was, but when I think about it, I wish she had said no to me and made me go back home to my parents, so I wouldn't have made all those mistakes that came with living with her. I wish Tonya hadn't bought those alcoholic drinks for me and told me that they made me an adult, when I was only fourteen years old. I wish she had been the kind of friend who wanted what was really best for me, and not what *I* said I thought was best for me.

As you get older, friends are the people who will share with you, even when they only have just a little more than you. In my life, those were friends like Neek, Shanetta, Tonya sometimes, and my Aunt Sheryl. I remember those days when I had stolen milk and diapers for Zion and I didn't want to take anything else. I would go for days without eating and Shanetta, Neek, and Tonya would give me five dollars, so I could go get a good meal, like a double cheeseburger, fries, and a drink from Steak 'N' Shake. I remember Aunt Sheryl would also give me money or bring me a meal with meat and vegetables. The way they shared with me showed that they were real friends; they saw my circumstances and gave to me even when they heard me say I didn't need it. Now I don't have to worry about eatin', but I do still have to worry that my soul is being fed and that is what my friends do for me now. Sometimes it is just allowing me to be my old self without the expectation of me being different even though my lifestyle is different. I need to be able to watch TV at home with Tonya or Neek and be able to talk about how cute the guys are and how fly their cars are without anyone mentioning that now I have the car I want or now I have the house I want. Just allowing me to escape from my new reality is like the five-dollar burger they used to provide. My friends now just need to let me be me. Every stage in my life has brought on new needs and expectations from my real friends. I pray to God that I won't ever need a five-dollar cheeseburger brought to me when I haven't eaten in days, but what fills me up is just knowing that Neek and Aunt Sheryl would bring it to me, if I ever needed it, and not even mention what I used to have and that I let it get away from me. They get props from me because our friendship allows us to grow and fall and get back up and through it all, we are the same.

I also eventually learned what a friend is *not*. Someone who is not a friend is someone who will talk about you behind your back or a person who would take from you when they know you don't have much. A person who is not a real friend may also hit or harm you. When I was younger, "hit or harm" referred to physical actions, but now that I have grown, I realize that people who are your friends would never hurt or harm your reputation by saying anything that would be damaging to you or your career. A real friend would never physically hurt you, of course, but more importantly they would never hurt your chances of progressin' and takin' it to the next level. A real friend knows what your dreams for yourself are, and they would do anything they could to help you reach your goals, whether they are professional or personal. That is what true friendship is.

• • •

I have to say that my experience with friendships may be unique, because I have had this crazy experience of leaving home to go sing, and so much of my life changed as a result of winning this singing competition. I have the unique situation of becoming "famous" in my late teens and early twenties, when all maturing adults are learning what real friendship is. To be honest, the past year has taken a toll on my friendships, which is something that happens to everyone who goes through a big life change. Events like this just show you who your real friends are, and they show you who was never your friend in the first place. The people who weren't your friends before and want to be your friends now are always the ones to avoid at all times!

My real friends have stuck around and stood behind me during all of it. And now that I have this "fame" thing, they call me just like nothing ever happened. Even though I may have a new phone number and a new cell phone number, they can still call me just like they always did, just like they did when I lived in the Farmington Apartments. I may not be home as much, my house might be a little bigger, but when they get me—they get ME. My real friends call and ask the same things, like who I'm datin', what does he look like? And what shoes have I bought lately? They tell me about their baby daddies and what's going on in Farmington and the new shoes they saw at the mall. It is just like it always was. My true friends have my back. My true friends want to know all about what I'm doing on the road besides singin'. My true friends don't envy me—they just see my new work as a new job that takes a lot out of me. They see me as having a job that includes signing thousands of autographs. My real friends care about me and ask if I'm getting enough rest. My real friends know that sometimes I can't call them just because I'm catching up on sleep or just trying to have a moment of peace. My real friends know that singin' is my dream come true. My real friends are happy for me.

Speakin about "real friends," even my family can't believe that Toya is still my best friend. Toya is my friend from back in the day. She is from Orangeburg, South Carolina—the deep country. Toya used to be wild, and she used to fight all the time. Toya first met Kima and they used to hang out together. One time, we all went out together and Toya and I realized we were very much alike. We laughed loudly and we were both real. Toya and I started doing a bunch of things together, like getting drunk and going out to meet men or just hanging out at home. We got loud when we got together. People could hear us and feel us a mile away. Toya and I were known as the party girls of High Point.

The thing I love about Toya is that although my life started to change I didn't have to pretend to be any way with her. She was just the truth all the time. She never pretended about nothin'. When she was broke, she would say it. When she had a new man, she told me about him, not worrying that I would take him. When she didn't have a new man and needed one, she would say, "I am lookin' for a man tonight." She was just so *real* and that allowed me to be real, free, and myself with her. Toya always knew the real me and even

though my circumstances have changed, she knows that
'Tasia is still in here no matter what. That is why Toya didn't
mind being her loud self backstage at Jay Leno's show. Jay
Leno doesn't mean anything to her, and I love that about her,
because just when I am thinkin' "Jay Leno" means something, Toya reminds me that he is just a person with a job,
just like me.

Toya and I still have the same friendship we had before
the madness of *Idol.* Toya has my back and I have hers. I
never had a sister, and so she does all the things that a sister
would do. Toya has been through some things similar to me,
like dropping out of school, and she, too, is only twenty-one
years old. When we are together now we can talk about God
and her experience with church. Toya and I have laughed
and cried together. Toya is my "dog." She is so strong and I
admire her. She has recently gone back to school.

I will never forget that during *Idol,* Toya called me and
said, "Dang, dog, you are doing your thing on TV." She
wanted to tell me that because I was doin' my thing, she was
doing hers by goin' back to school.

Although Toya can be ghetto and loud, she is very smart
and her daughter Shnaya thinks she is the best mama ever.
Being with Toya just keeps me knowing where I come from,
without shame. I am proud of where I come from when I am
with Toya. I salute her. We have grown *together,* not apart.

As you can see all of my friends except for my brother
are women. I think that is true for most women. I guess it is

still very hard for me to trust men. I think trust is hard for most of the women I have known in my life. Many of the people I know have not had good male role models in our lives or any decent romantic relationships, for that matter. Many of us have had our fathers abandon our families, and our mothers are full of hate toward the men who left them. If the men stayed around they were cheatin' on their wives or not even marrying the mothers of their children at all. Seein' all these things has trained many women to choose the wrong men, who always end up doin' us wrong. It's a bad cycle. It's sad to say, but many of us don't even know the difference between a good man and a bad one. We think that a good one is the one who can say the right things and looks the best. I have learned that words are cheap, and the things that men can say to us don't mean anything without the actions that back them up. I keep trying to have a good relationship with men, and I now realize that trust is the main factor that is lacking in me and making my relationships hard.

But trusting people is the hardest thing to do because you never really know them until they have shown their feelings with their actions. Actions always speak louder than words. And actions still can never tell the whole story. That's another reason that life is not a fairy tale. You just have to live it and trust in God to put you in the right place and the right time with the right person.

Honestly, this is one of the hardest lessons that I need to

learn and I'm still workin' on it. But I just keep tryin' and everyone I meet who disappoints me just makes me stronger and able to see more clearly the next time. It's not easy. As I told you, I fall in love easily—but I'm more choosy now, and that's a good thing.

You just have to keep God's love at the center of your heart. And if one person disappoints you, you have to keep lovin' until you meet the person who doesn't disappoint you. If you stay mad at all the people who have wronged you, you will not be able to open up your heart to someone new and receive what they have for you—which may be what you want. Women like us, who have been though a lot, truly deserve to get what we are looking for. We too need our props.

MY MOMENT OF
FAITH: WHAT I LEARNED

My flesh and my heart faileth; but God is the strength of my heart, and my portion for ever.

PSALMS 73:26

- Be your own friend.
- If God is for you, who could be against you?

While I am givin' props, I just have to give props to the following singers who have inspired me in so many ways.

New Singers

- **Tweet**—I admire her voice. She has the voice of a songbird. She has a song like no other.
- **Beyoncé**—Beyoncé is very creative. She has one of those voices that stand out and you know it's her. You hear one of her songs and you know, "That's B!"
- **India.Arie**—India has such a soulful voice and beautiful voice control. I love her subjects and how she looks at life and the way she expresses her feelings in all her songs. And I love her style!

Gospel

- **Kierra "Kiki" Sheard**—Kiki is a sixteen-year-old gospel singer. She reminds me a lot of me because she started when she was young too. She is the daughter of one of the gospel Clark Sisters. Kiki is an anointed little girl and I love her. She is simply a baad, anointed sister. She is a *"baad mamma jamma!"* She's hot!

Divas

- **Angela Bassett**—She is so beautiful.
- **Mo'Nique**—She is a big woman and a good role model for me because she knows that she is fine and she doesn't care what anybody thinks. Mo'Nique has it *"goin' on."*

Legends

- **Billie Holiday and Ella Fitzgerald**—They both had the kind of voices that can do what the instruments do.

It was Ella who started runs—she showed what you can do with your vocal. I still listen to them today and I'm young! It's music that's legendary. Their music will always be around.

- **Aretha Franklin**—She is my favorite singer. She has a voice like no other. I have to say that I have been blessed enough to meet Miss Aretha Franklin. She has wanted to get to know me better. She has given me her phone number and it just sits until I'm ready to call her. I'm not ready yet. After a couple of months, I went to my mother and I said, "Mama, I can't call Aretha." My mother said, "Why not? Just talk to her!" And I said, "You can't just *talk* to Aretha!"

  I love you, Aretha! And that's why I haven't called you yet.

7. Like **Mother,**
Like **Daughter**

The highest props for my success go out to my mother. Diane Barrino is my biggest role model. She is my angel. My mother is my guide and my friend. We are almost the same person. I can tell her anything and she doesn't judge me. We never judge each other. We both have done it all, lost it all, found out what we were made of, and managed to change our lives. And we are both still standin'.

I come from a long line of strong women who have kept their heads up through a lot of adversity and hardship. My grandmother, Addie, was born on Christmas morning in 1941 in Bennettsville, South Carolina. Her mother, my great-grandmother, died from bronchial asthma at the age of thirty-two when Addie was only eight years old. She had told Addie that she was going to the doctor to see about her asthma and sinus infection and never came home. She died in the doctor's office. Addie moved in with her aunt and uncle, who took good care of her and made sure she was raised right. My grandmother was raised in the church and got saved when she was fifteen years old while attending Oak Grove Mississippi Baptist Church. She also became the first victim of our "generational curse," as my mother calls it, by having children too young, but at least Addie was married. My grandmother married my grandfather, Neil Washington, at nineteen years old and had her first child and namesake, Addie, at twenty.

Over the years, Addie had two more daughters, my mother, Diane, and Surayda, the youngest. But, my mother told me, like so many of the men in my history, Neil was an alcoholic and he was abusive throughout my grandparents' marriage. Although Addie was going to church and doing all of her regular activities with a smile on her face, she was constantly covering up bruises, which were the result of Neil's beatings. He would blacken her eyes right before prayer meetin', so she had to go to church with a face full of crusty makeup, trying to hide her swollen eyes and busted lips. As scared as my grandmother was of Neil's rages, she felt she needed to honor her marriage vows, which were made before God—she took her promise seriously. She also did not want to disappoint her beloved aunt who had raised her. But Neil's abuse got worse—any little thing would set him off. If Addie didn't make his dinner just right, or the house wasn't just right when he came home, he would beat her. After a while, he didn't need a reason, and he beat her in front of her girls. Addie was convinced that one of Neil's punches would eventually kill her and leave her precious daughters with a man who might hurt them, too. But Addie never left him. It was Neil, not my grandmother, who finally broke the cycle of violence. After fourteen years of marriage, he asked Addie for a divorce with the soured smell of liquor on his breath.

Addie finally had the escape she had wanted but had been unwilling to bring on herself. God had intervened. Addie heard those words from her husband, "I want a divorce," and realized that she could raise her daughters on her own. Addie decided to move with the girls to High Point, where she had family who could help her. She didn't have a plan and she didn't have much money, but she had a faith in God that was unshakable. And she knew that after living through fourteen years of hell, she and her girls would survive.

My grandmother had a dream for each of her daughters. My grandma says that my aunt Addie, the eldest, was "all business," even as a young girl. Aunt Addie was on a mission to get out of High Point as soon as she could, and so she eventually attended the Wilma Boyd Career School in Pennsylvania. My grandmother was so proud because it is exactly what she wanted. Aunt Addie graduated, took a job in Dallas, and never looked back.

Aunt Surayda, the youngest, was also ambitious, and my grandmother had high hopes for her, too. Rayda wanted to

get her certification and become a registered nurse. Unfortunately she never got the chance. Two weeks before the start
of her first nursing job, a stranger came to Surayda's house,
calling out her boyfriend's name. When she opened the door
to say that he wasn't there and she hadn't heard from him in
a while, the man opened fire and shot her in the neck.
Surayda fell dead in front of her daughters, Kima and Kadijah, who screamed over their dead mother's body. The mur-
derer was never caught. My grandmother says, "I am still
living with that." She has never gotten over the death of her
baby girl.

My grandmother had dreams for her middle daughter,
too. She had hoped that my mother, Diane, would find happiness in her gift of music and arranged for her to interview
at music schools and possibly earn a scholarship. Addie
pushed Diane to focus on school, but Diane chose love, marriage, and having her own family. Mama's love for Daddy and
the birth of her first son, Rico, changed her mind about education and singing. It just wasn't that important to her anymore. Addie still says Diane giving up her dreams devastated
her, but she also says, "I did get Diane with the church." To
this day, my grandma says that my mama was the daughter
who was always with her at church. Mama was always sensitive to the Spirit. That spiritual thread runs through all of the
women in my family, but especially through my mother and
me. I pray I can pass it on to Zion.

As my grandmother used to say about mothers like
mine, "She makes a way out of no way." And all those nights

when we didn't have enough to eat or enough electricity or enough heat, we always had a song in our hearts and a smile on our faces. That is because of the things that my mother was able to give us. Although my brothers love my mother to death, there is something mysterious and unseen that ties her and me together so tightly. It is more than love between us. It is not just the fact that we look so much alike. It is not the fact that we both love shoes and fashion. It is not that we love God above all else. It is that our souls are the *same*. We have had the same circumstances. We have made the same mistakes. We have both hurt our mothers and in some ways we are both trying to make up for it—my mother became a minister and I became the star that her mother wanted her to be.

Mama is my biggest role model. She is my guide and my friend. I can tell my mother anything and she doesn't judge me. We never judge each other. We both have done some crazy things. We are standin' proud because of how far we have come. But no matter how far I rise, my mother will always be my angel, looking out for me.

In fact, "I need an angel" is the name that is programmed into my cell phone instead of "Mama." Every time Mama calls me, I am reminded of what I need most in my life: Diane Barrino.

I have never seen my mother do anything wrong. But that's because I was born after she had turned her life around. The truth is my mother, like me, used to do *everything* wrong. She partied, she drank, and she smoked—just like me. Just like many young girls from the church who are told that all those things are so wrong. Don't get me wrong, Grandma Addie tried to keep my mother in line, but she rebelled. She wanted to experience everything. We both did. When Diane said she was going to the park, she would usually wind up somewhere else that meant trouble. I guess that's how Mama ended up seeing my daddy on those nights when they weren't supervised. My mother fell in love with a boy from the church and got pregnant with a kid when she was just a kid herself. I did the same thing.

These mistakes that we both made are nothin' to be proud of. But these experiences are the root of where we come from. The excitement of rebellion and the pain of irreversible mistakes are what have made us the women that we are today. And in spite of the embarrassment, pain, fear, and humiliation that we have both endured from the world, the church, and our men, we are still standing tall and that is what keeps our heads up.

In order to fully understand 'Tasia and how she has kept her head up, you have to understand Mama and who she is. I want to tell you about her because without understandin' her, there is no understandin' me.

My mother is a very caring woman. She is the most generous person I have ever met. Her kindness to others is the thing I think of most when I think of her. I believe that trait has been passed to me as well. When my brothers were growing up, there was always someone whose mother put their son out of the house. They put them out because of those teenage fits that young men go through. It was the usual High Point dramas: girls, pregnancies, not workin', bein' lazy, bein' messy, drinkin', smokin', and not goin' to school. They were all the things that my brothers were going through too, but they were never put out of our house. My mama would never do that. During a particularly terrible fight with Daddy, he had put her out of her own house, so she knew personally how it felt to be on the street. Grandma Addie used to tell Mama, "There's nothing worse than not having a place to go." Those boys, my brother's friends, knew they could always come to our house even when there was no guarantee that *our* family would be eatin' that night. My mother always told those boys that they could stay with us. She used to say, "You just lay down on that couch, take this blanket, and stay as long as you want." Mama was just *carin'*.

She passed that carin' to my heart like a torch. Now, I'm like that, too. We both can't help helpin' people, in whichever way we can. So now, years later, I have helped my brothers with their child-support payments, I have bought Tiny a car, I have given my mother a car and started her first bank account. I can't help wantin' to help. If I could help everybody in the world, I would. Now, my mother sees me helpin' everybody and she warns me by saying, "Fantasia, you're just like me. You want to help everybody, but you can't." She is probably right, but I learned it from her. I guess I want to be somebody's angel someday, too.

My mother is a true mother. We kids go to her with every need. It's as if we think she is the smartest woman in the world. As her kids, we think that, but it is not true. My mother, like me, didn't graduate from high school, yet we go to her with our health and our legal problems, our spiritual dilemmas, just everything. When I am sick on the road, I call and tell her that I'm sick. She says with her soothing voice, "I'm going to get out there to take care of you." She books a flight for herself and Zion and comes to wherever I am. Knowing that they are on their way makes me feel better even before they arrive. She gives me her homemade remedies and I'm miraculously healed. I remember one time she came to my rescue when I thought I was losing my voice. She brought some tea and honey with lemon and whiskey. She called it a hot toddy. Mama rubbed my neck with Vick's ointment and wrapped my neck and chest with white hotel towels, and then put me to sleep with her humming a tune in my ear. I was able to sing the next morning.

As a teen mother of three before she was twenty, my mother has provided me with wisdom that you can't get in school or in books. She has taught me really important lessons that I take with me in everyday life. My mother's values continue to sustain me. I hope to pass these valuable life lessons that began with my grandmother, were passed on to my mother, and given to me to pass on to Zion—I only hope it won't take Zion so long to get it. And I hope that she won't have to make all kinds of terrible mistakes to realize that she should listen to me.

Mama always said, Respect yourself and others. My mother always tells me that she tried to be the kind of woman who would avoid certain situations that made her appear to be anything less than a good mother. Mama tells me this is because of the kind of mother she had in Addie. She tells me now, "If I ever drank a beer, you would have never known. I carried myself in a respectful way, just like my Mama did and just like you should at all times." She wanted us to always respect her. "I wanted y'all to be proud of me," she still says with tears in her eyes, fearing that we don't because of the mistakes she has made, like staying with Daddy after he cheated on and disrespected her. But I know now that she did the best that she knew how to do at the time.

Because my mother created such an image of who she was and still is, I use the same way of thinkin' toward Zion. I never want her to be able to say to me that she saw me in a compromising position, disrespecting myself. I make sure of that, even though I'm in an industry where sex sells. I work extra hard to be someone that my baby can emulate and be proud of, so that she can be proud of who she is. I want to have the freedom to tell Zion when she gets to be thirteen years old, "You ain't wearing that skirt." And Zion won't be able to look at me and say, "Why not? You were wearing it in that video you were doing." That's because her mama would have taught her to respect herself, just like my mama tried to teach me.

"Believe in God" was what my mother told me every single day of my life, because that was what her mama told her, but also because it was how she lived. My mother taught me from the womb about God. She taught me that God was something bigger than us and something bigger than the eye could see. My mom saw God in action when Aunt Surayda was killed and when Grandma Addie almost lost her mind from the grief of it all. Grandma Addie carried the loss of Surayda in her heart, mind, and body. My mother thought she would lose her mother, too. But Grandma Addie got through it by asking God to take the pain away. She asked Him to lift the pain—and He did. Within a few weeks Grandma Addie was able to carry on with her life and raise Aunt Surayda's two daughters, who needed her. Mama saw God in action and that's why she always told me to enlist God in my battles and He will make everything better. And I have seen it happen in my own life time and time again.

Mama also taught me how to pray. Prayer was instilled in me just like the principles of right and wrong. It was just something that we did, *often*. And I always remember that she would say, "Although, you don't see the results right away, keep the faith. Faith will give you peace beyond understanding." Mama said that God was the man who is behind the scenes to keep us going. After those initial talks about God, I still have Him with me behind the scenes, on the stage, and in my heart at all times. One of the things that I love about my mother is that she continues to be a prayin' mom. I love that her prayers keep a shield over all her kids. But I never knew until I grew up how much praying to God Mama had to do to survive the many hardships her family had gone through. She prayed through her mother's pain, then her own, and finally her children's. She is always on her knees prayin' for us. And I believe in my heart that God answers prayers.

Grandma Addie always said, "Have hope and faith and things will work out." My mother believes it too. "Just hold on" is what my mother used to tell me, and "Believe in yourself," regardless of the circumstances. She would say, "Believe that things will always get better." That is what she used to tell me as she looked in the refrigerator and there was nothing to eat except for grits for the third day in a row. I remember my mother going with a friend to get the government-supplied free groceries. She would come home with cheese, powered milk, and peanut butter. My mother used to take the cheese that came in a long cardboard box and make the following dinners: cheese and eggs, cheese and grits, rice and cheese, and cheese sandwiches. Because she was serving it with a smile at the same time, she was a living example of the power of "holdin' on." I know now that faith was the only thing that kept my family going through the hardest times. I also know that without hope and faith in troubled times, there would be no reason to go on. When we were eating cheese and grits, or worse, every day, we might have given up without our faith to sustain us. I believe that God has a plan for each of us and we must keep our faith strong so that we are still here to see what He has in store.

Mama used to tell me to always maintain my inner strength, which is what Addie taught her. When I was a small girl and wondering how I would make it through the hardships of low self-esteem in a world that believes in beauty above all else, even above God, my mother would say, "You are stronger than you know. You can make it." My mother believed in me, even when I didn't believe in myself. And all those days that I cried and she just kept telling me about my gift, she was right. But Mama needed her inner strength when she thought I had thrown away my gift by getting pregnant. I floundered but found mine when I finally accepted that B. was wrong for me and used that strength to turn away from him. All of the women in my family have tremendous inner strength, and all of that strength has been tested many times over and we're still here. It is my inner strength that made it possible for me to go to the *American Idol* auditions—not wearing the right clothes and just holding my gift in my pocket. Mama said I could make it, and I did.

One of my grandmother's favorite sayings is "God's forgiveness is the key to freedom." My mother is the most forgiving woman I know. She has tried to teach this lesson to me, but it's been a difficult one to learn. It still amazes me as I watch my mother still being civil to my father and living under the same roof and still calling him her husband. Mama is a living testimony of forgiveness. There were so many years that she didn't smile or laugh for months at a time because her marriage was so hard. My mother once told me about her own marriage, "I got married because it was my decision. It was a disgrace to have children and no husband. I know; I did it too young. I guess I was sixteen when I was pregnant with Rico, and it was not quite a year when Joseph was born.

I got married and tried to grow up a little too fast. I should have waited and gotten a degree and gone back to school or something. I made the decision and decided if it didn't last but a week, I could say I was married."

My mother forgave herself for the choices that she made and therefore never demanded that I get married when I got pregnant. She once wrote me a letter that said, "Fantasia, I didn't want to push you to go back to school, but I didn't want to rush you into marriage either. Too young, I had to be a mother and wife. And I didn't want that for you. I wanted you to believe that you could have a second chance. I wanted you to do something that you would *decide to do*. I was embarrassed because I got pregnant a second time and my mother told me that was a disgrace. I got married because of my upbringing, but I don't want you to marry for that reason. I want you to forgive yourself and move on with your life." I love my mother because she is in the process of forgiving herself. Now I can see that Grandma Addie was right: forgiveness is the key to freedom, and in our own way both Mama and I are finally free.

Although we are mother and daughter and friends and tell each other most things, there are a few things that we have never said to each other or shared with the world. Because our connection is so strong, we have hopes and dreams for each other that are really for ourselves, because we are from the same root. What I wish for my mother is that she is always a blessed woman and that the pain and disappointment that her marriage has caused can slowly be washed away from her. I hope that she will always have nice things around her that make her happy. I also wish that my mother could see that there are good and trustworthy people in the world. My mother has been through so many things; her heart has hardened in some ways. She doesn't go out. She doesn't have any friends who she trusts. She has had friends steal from her, lie to her, and try to date her husband. My dream is to show my mother the wonderful people who I have met. I wish that I could introduce her to all of the Idols who were all from different places and were my friends. They were there for me. I want to show her that there are people in the world that you can trust. But most of all I wish Mama happiness, so that the smile that she used to have when Aunt Rayda was alive will return to her after all these years of grieving her loss.

My mother's wish for me was that I would break our family's generational curse. When I got pregnant, it was a mistake she had seen too many times in our family and that is not what she wanted for me. My grandmother still has hopes that I will finish high school, which is what she wanted for all three of her daughters. My aunts accomplished that goal and so did my grandmother—my mother and I did not. My mother wanted better for me and she knew I was really talented and loved people and she had big dreams for me. But she knows that I need to have an education to really be able to take care of myself and my daughter. She doesn't want me to focus on the negatives, like the fact that I can't read very well. She wants me to know that I'm not dumb;

I've just had some extra challenges in my life that have made me stronger. And I finally believe her. She wanted me to be everything that she didn't become and I'm working on it. She's got big dreams for me now—she wants to see me go to the Grammys because she never did. Next year, *I will.*

My mother says that I have matured a lot over the last few years. She is proud. She says that I matured after Zion was born. She also says that I matured after *American Idol* because I never lost myself with all the things that were goin' on and all the ways I could have fallen into the "Hollywood" trap of drinking and partying—just showing out. She knew the pressure that I was under and was a little worried about whether I could handle it all. But I continue to try and make her proud. Mama says that *American Idol* brought a lot of discipline to my life and brought me far enough to have goals and dreams, when before, I had none. She is also proud that I never forget where I came from. She always tells me to keep it real with myself and other people. She wants me to remain grateful for what I have and never forget that I can lose it as quickly as it came.

The torch has now been passed to me to raise my little girl like the women in my life have raised theirs, but hopefully without all of the drama and pain that lack of money causes. I feel scared because I don't think I'm in any way equal to the women that my mother and grandmother are.

For Zion, I will tell her that God should come first in her life. I will show her how God turned our life around because of the gift that God gave me to sing. I will tell Zion the stories of Montlieu Avenue and how I dropped out of school and what I have had to go through because I made that choice. Zion will know how to pray, like every woman in our family. I just pray that she will be praying for good grades, a good job, and a good man, not praying for bills to be paid or for the lights to stay on. Hopefully our family is through with those types of prayers.

I will teach Zion to forgive. But I hope she will not have to forgive a man for hurting her or stealing from her or leaving her alone with a baby. I hope that she will someday be able to forgive her daddy for abandoning her. I will tell her about disappointments in life and how we set certain expectations for the people we love and sometimes they don't do what we want them to do.

Zion will know about respecting others, because she will grow up in a world filled with music and cultures and people from all parts of the world. I will teach her to love and respect all people, but she will also learn from me how to respect herself. My hope for Zion is that she won't be a desperate woman. My prayer is that Zion will build herself up inside, so that there won't be any holes in her heart, needin' a man to fill. I will teach her to fill herself with God.

The last thing that I will teach Zion is to have inner strength. I want her to have the kind of strength that Addie and Mama had, and that I have had at times. All of us have had the strength to keep going no matter what happened to us. No matter how cruel life can be, I want Zion to be a survivor.

• • •

My mother was excited that I wanted to write a chapter about her. She wanted the chapter to be in my own words like the rest of the book, but she was dyin' to get in somewhere. So, I told her, Mama, you can put in your moments of faith. Her moments got us to this moment.

DIANE'S MOMENT OF
FAITH: WHAT SHE LEARNED

Train up a child in the way he should go: and when he is old, he will not depart from it.

PROVERBS 22:6

- My prayer was always that this poverty be broken for my family. I believe that God used Fantasia to break the generational barrier of poverty.
- When you have children they all have their own personalities. Your children may not be what you want them to be, because they have their own personalities.
- God's favor goes further than money.
- Fantasia still wants to go to Wal-Mart every time she's at home. She calls it Wally World. And when she's there, she never hesitates to stop to take pictures or sign autographs. She feels like she has been given such an enormous gift to be in this position, so if they want a picture they deserve it. She feels like she owes the world.

- When it came to church, Fantasia was unique in that she didn't just sing, she sang with an anointing. She would go into a crazy praise and everyone would be looking at her, wondering what was wrong with her. I often said it came from the womb. Fantasia would take on worship that would take people to a whole 'nother level in spirit.

8. It Ain't About the Bling

When I won *Idol,* it was like a dream come true—but there were strings attached that I hadn't even thought about. The dream part was that there were 65 million people who decided that I was the best singer in the competition and voted for me. That part was wonderful. But the newfound money part has not been easy for me. Now I know you're thinkin' that should be the easiest part of winning, but the truth is that I struggle with the enormous change in this area of my life. I struggle with it every single day.

My mother used to say to us about the poor financial decisions we made, "Y'all make bad decisions. You don't plan for things; you just do things without a plan and then you are nowhere." Then Mama would shake her head regretfully and say, "That's what usually happens to people who come from nothin' and suddenly have more money than they thought they could." Today my mother says that she is sorry for us all because we never saw anyone who had real money and now we don't know how to act when we do have money.

As you know, my family struggled every step of the way. It was a struggle to get Christmas gifts every year and that was even in the years when my parents had jobs. Some years, Christmas gifts were not even talked about. Some years, my family struggled so much that singin' was the only gift we got.

Singin' was all we knew. We were always trying to catch a hustle by performing anywhere we could. When you have had a life like that, money is always a short-lived reward for just being somewhere and giving a song. There was never enough money to accumulate or save. When you got it, you spent it and that's just the way it was. When we would perform, the money we got was just enough to pay for that evening's dinner or the gas to get back home. We weren't even livin' paycheck to paycheck like some folks; we were livin' dollar to dollar.

And all those years we still took our music seriously because we felt that getting money just to sing was a blessing. The singing made us feel like we were ten feet tall. The cash was just gravy. Sadly, all that has changed for me now. Now that money and material things have entered my life, I don't feel as rich just being near the music as I did before. Now I feel like, even though I have so much more than I ever thought I would, it's not enough. Makin' music is no longer just an honor. Now I feel like the music is work and I deserve to be paid for my work. I see now that having more money makes you need and need more and more money. The more you have the more you think you need. I have gained some money, but I think I lost something valuable—I have forgotten how to be happy with what I have.

My whole family is strugglin' with money just as we always were, but in a different way. We're struggling to understand real money—not just "gas money," not just "dinner money," but *real* money that is enough to accumulate and save and invest. None of us have ever had it like that and that is why we are so confused about how to be with this new wealth of ours. We have been in need of things for so long that it's hard to change our way of thinking, especially when it seems we can get what we want so easily.

Diamonds, luxury cars, and too many clothes are so tempting to me. All I can think of is all those years I didn't have nice clothes to wear. All I can think of is all those years that I felt so ugly and poor and not dressed well enough. All I can think of is those girls with new clothes on the first day of school every year and my shame of my summer-worn clothes from last year. But I get scared of shopping too much, because I would never stop if I started. I feel like I could spend everything I had on clothes just to wash away those childhood memories. I think the reason my family is now spending so much money is because they are trying to buy their way out of their past.

When I'm thinkin' clear, I know I don't want to be broke. I don't want to be just another "famous girl" tryin' to forget the past so hard that I act a fool and waste all that I have on material goods. After all the past is what brought me and my family to this point. I am just sayin' a prayer that God will guide me. I also ask God that He touch the hearts of my family and let them see the possibilities of saving and investing and not be blinded by the bling.

Having money has always been a subject that makes people uncomfortable. Like the rap song says, "Mo' money, mo' problems." *That is the truth.* When you have always had nothin', you don't expect as much. Your expectations are as simple as your current lifestyle. If your only concern is having enough to eat and payin' your rent and you don't own anything, your only goal is just to make it day to day, or week to week, or month to month. That's not an easy life, but it's a pretty simple one, and it's one that most people I know live every day.

The hip-hop bling-bling culture is based on livin' the millionaire life or at least lookin' like you live the millionaire life. And with all these hip-hop and pop songs talking about "millions" in every verse, everyone seems to always be thinking about getting as much money as they can. How much money you get is the first thing people think about with fame and celebrity. I hate to break the news, but just because a person has fame and celebrity, you can't assume they are anywhere close to having a million dollars. I bet you're assuming that I have millions, but, trust me, that ain't the truth.

First of all, as a winner on *American Idol*, I can tell you that everyone is interested about what the winner wins. The winner of the show does get a million-dollar record deal, but does not get a million dollars in cash as some people think. Most people don't understand the actual numbers behind the music business at all. You must be wondering why there is a whole chapter about money. Because what I have realized is that news of my winning automatically leads people to thinkin' about money. I hate the thought that money might make us who we are, but the sad news is that, all too often in this world, it seems that it does.

What makes me laugh about it is that the Barrino Family never had money. All we had was music, good singing voices, and an anointing from God. Mama used to say, "Money is the root of all evil." I'm beginning to think she may be right. Don't get me wrong; I'm grateful for many of the things that this newfound money has brought me. But I also feel guilty getting caught up in this money thing, when I never meant to. It's like a tidal wave. Maybe that's why so many of us never wanted to do much in High Point. With success comes money, and that can be scary when you come from where I do. Everyone in the ghetto talks about wantin' money and gettin' money and makin' money, but if they ever were to make some real money they wouldn't know how to manage it and then they would still end up with nothing, but it would be twice as hard to go back to not having any money.

Why is it that when we have money we feel like we can

have more things? That makes us feel like we're better than people who don't have money or who have fewer things. People put too much power in money for it to be such a fleeting thing. Money don't last. You can have money one day and lose it the next. You can lose it in a card game or a stupid bet or you can lose it in a slot machine with just one pull of a lever. That is the evil of money. Why are we not as equally obsessed with God, who is lasting and almighty? Why has money replaced God as the most important thing? I'm blessed by what God has given me and my family, but this money thing continues to worry me.

For those who think that I'm now livin' large, this is an example of what happens to large sums of money, based on my own experience.

You always have to begin with taxes and management fees, so now you're looking at less than half of what you started with. I decided I wanted a house. My family has always rented houses, so it has always been my dream to own a house for us to live in, a house that we could really call our own. I also understood that buying a home was a better investment than spending my money on a luxury car that I couldn't drive or diamonds that I probably wouldn't wear. I liked the idea of spending my money on something I believe in and that is home! So now my whole family lives in a beautiful house that I bought in Charlotte, North Carolina. This is a great blessing for us and I love goin' home every chance I get. I also love calling it "my home" because owning a home of my own was a dream that I couldn't even imagine just a short while ago.

Of course, I have monthly bills just like everybody else. We all have to pay the utility bills, put dinner on the table, pay for insurance, and pay for all those minutes that we spend talking on the phone. But when you're in the public eye, you suddenly have expenses that you never even thought about like security, hairstylists, and assistants. And one of the blessings of having some money in my pocket is getting to do what I love best (next to singin') and that is helpin' people. I've helped my family by buying them new cars and givin' them a place to live. I've paid off their bills and given them some things that they always wanted. And I've helped friends by giving them spending money to buy things they really want. I tithe every week, and I always have some money in my pocket so I can help those in need. I believe in givin' back.

It gives me a good feeling that I can do things for Mama and my brother Xavier. It makes me feel good that Xavier goes to a good school. I want him to have every advantage possible in life so he can go on to college. I want Xavier to be "cool," handsome, and *smart*—which he already is. I want him to be a workin' man with a few dollars in his pocket. I don't want him to be hustlin' with the neighborhood boys hangin' out at the gas station, waitin' to make trouble. Xavier is better than that. He was raised right and for once, one of Mama's kids will choose right, even if it is with a little help from me. It makes me smile to be able to give him the schoolin' he needs to help himself become a good man who knows how to be productive and prosper. Because Mama takes care of Zion for me, I feel that I should help her with raising Xavier, because she can't go out and make money on her own anymore. It's like that saying: "Give a man a fish, and you have fed him for today. Teach a man to fish, and you have fed him for a lifetime." I would like to teach Xavier and my whole family to fish.

So for all of you who think that I'm sittin' around countin' my millions just because I won *American Idol*, I'm here to tell ya livin' large just means that you need more money and it brings bigger money worries. Y'all know I'm tellin' it all, because I want to set the record straight. I've taken on a lot to take care of my family and I have to work every single day to continue to have enough for all of them.

Also, because I didn't write any of the songs on my first album, my income from the record sales is less than that of artists who do write their own songs. However, I look forward to collaborating on songs in the future. And all artists have to pay management-related fees. I don't mean to tell my business like that, but people ask me about it all the time and everybody waits for me to pay when they are with me. I also need to understand the reality of the money situation for myself. I struggle every day with keeping my promise to my family and keeping my promise to myself, which was to make it with my music and not ever have to go without again.

Since I won *American Idol*, nothing is the same. It seems

RIGHT: *As soon as you make it on the show, you start posing for "celeb" photos. Look how sweet I look!*

BELOW: *This is the picture that started it all—the first Polaroid of me at the* American Idol *auditions.*

Getting beautiful backstage.

Sharin' my gift.

RIGHT: *Huggin' up to Ryan.*

MIDDLE: *Hangin' with the girls backstage—La Toya, Diana, Jasmine, and a member of the production team.*

BELOW: *It starts to seem real in the final three.*

Singing to win, reaching to God with the choir behind me.

I can taste it now!

The moment my dreams came true.

Cheesin' to the camera like an Idol with Daddy and Zion.

Four generations of Barrino women.

Celebratin' the win with my daughter, my brothers, and my friends.

My miracle house. Look how far I've come!

Everyone wants to congratulate me on my win. Even the UPS man wants a hug!

I'm in trouble! Zion showing off her 'Tasia attitude.

like one day I was hanging out in High Point and the next day I was being taken around by a Realtor looking at houses that I never thought I would be able to see the inside of, much less be able to buy one and own it.

I think my problem has always been thinking that having material things would make me happy. I think my whole family and all of the people from home have the same problem. What I'm realizing is that money and things don't make you happy. All things really can do for you is make you more comfortable. And comfort is *not* happiness.

Now that I have a little money, I'm noticing that money seems to mean everything to almost everybody I know. I guess it always has been this way, but being involved with real money for the first time and seeing how it complicates things, I'm now standing back and appreciating the little things in life. The simplest and most important thing in my life is Zion. Unfortunately, I haven't been able to spend a lot of time with her since all of this has happened. So, just by being with her, having her fall asleep in my room or in my lap makes me feel like the richest and happiest woman in the world. It's her deep need for me and my being there that makes priceless moments.

Zion has taught me a lot about happiness. And even though I once believed that having material things would make us both happy, I learned from Zion's deep brown eyes that when I would give her a new doll or a new toy or a pink canopy bed for her princess room, and then said I have to go away again, the canopy, the new dolls, and the new toys suddenly didn't mean anything to her. Her eyes said it all. All she wanted was for me to stay with her. And when I saw that look in her eyes, I realized those material things really didn't mean anything to me, either. I have to admit that I did spend money on Zion. I had a big need for Zion, and I wanted her to have new clothes, not hand-me-downs. I wanted her to have more than two pretty pink church dresses so she could choose from several. I wanted her to have shiny new patent leather shoes for church. I wanted her to have matching bows for her hair. I wanted my baby to have a winter coat like they have in the baby magazines. I wanted Zion to feel like a princess. I know I'm probably overdoing it with Zion, but what I want for her most above all else is pride, the one thing that I didn't have when I was comin' up. I wanted Zion to have all the things that I always wanted and never had. That may have been selfish in a way, but it just made me feel better that as a single parent I was trying to provide all the things that were missing. I see now that buying all those things for Zion was for me only. Now I'm much more aware of what to give Zion. I don't buy her things every time I miss her or am feeling guilty about being away. Now I only give her what she needs, like a call every night to say good night. That makes her much happier and it makes me happier than anything I could buy.

Other little things in life, like walking on the beach and admiring the magnitude of the ocean, makes me see God's power. The fact that I'm still breathing and waking up every day and being able to get myself up and moving is a blessing.

I thank God for the financial rewards now, but I have so much more than that to be thankful for.

Now I want to be *wise* so I can still take care of myself and not have to rely on just money to make everything happen. Wisdom is not what is expected from celebrities or recording artists who came from nothing. They expect us to get money and spend it all up on furs, cars, diamonds, and mansions. All that crazy stuff in the videos.

People ask me what I spend my money on, and I tell them that it is important to me to take care of my family. I have been asked, "Why do you feel you have to do it?" It's not that I have to do it, but I want to do it because it's the promise that we made to each other on Montlieu Avenue just a few short years ago. I just happen to be the one who got blessed first. We were all in it together—my mama and daddy and brothers, we were all travelin' and singin'. That's all we did for most of my childhood. At times, we all slept in the same dark room together. We ate grits, bacon, eggs, bologna, and corned beef hash for days at a time for breakfast, lunch, and dinner. We *struggled* together, and although we were young, my brothers and I had grown-folk struggles. When we had no hot water in the house, we used to yell down to the kitchen, "Boil me some water so I can bathe!" Everybody used to huddle up together to keep warm when there was no heat. When I think back to those days, it brings tears to my eyes. My tears are tears of joy because we survived and we never have to be out of heat or water and now we all have our own rooms. I was the youngest, but I would always say, "Man, one day we're going to make it! Watch when one of us gets somethin' and we're not going to have to go through this anymore." *I meant that.* We were normal kids: We wanted to go places and we wanted to have things. All of those memories of growing up remind me of *wanting*. That much wanting *hurts*.

As crazy as it sounds, even if I hadn't made that promise to my family, I would still be doing exactly the same thing I'm doing for them, because I would be lost without them. They are all that I have ever had. My house was meant to be filled with family. That's why we all worked so hard to have something; it wasn't only my efforts. It just turns out that I made it first. By giving the prize to me, it was really for all the Barrinos as a reward for all those years of strugglin' together. My brothers missed out on basketball and football games, proms and nights out at the drive-in. I missed out on joining the cheerleading squad and track meets. We missed out on everything that most kids our age were able to do because we were out singin' and performin' and trying to satisfy our hunger for music.

My situation with my family is not without problems. It is hard enough to be me, wanting so much that I never had before. Imagine a whole family that has never had anything and now being able to give them what they really want and need, in addition to my own wants and needs. I'm trying to get my family to see that it really ain't about the bling, but that is a hard thing to show people when the bling is all that they have ever dreamed about.

My family has very little formal education and only now are we starting to see the light about how important education is. My father is a certified truck driver. My grandmother's husband, Ray, got him a job with his trucking company so that he could take care of his family. My mother started her nursing education, became a certified nursing technician (CNT) but never stayed in school so she could become a registered nurse. Because our family has such a passion and talent for music, it has always been that we are a little stubborn about working in other areas that don't involve music. Of course my parents had to do other things because they had mouths to feed, but my father did manage to get us involved in music despite his trucking job, and despite the fact that we should have all been in school learnin', but more than anything else, he just wanted us to sing. As the kids in my family have all have grown up, we honestly didn't, and still don't, have much interest in anything that doesn't involve music.

Whenever I come home to Charlotte or High Point, my cell phone constantly rings with people giving me a list of needs, wants, and loan requests. My problem is that I always end up giving what they ask for, but it stresses me out, because I can't afford to do all the things that everyone wants for much longer. It seems no matter what I say, it continues to be the same thing, more calls asking for more things. I was trying to help them so that they could help themselves, but it isn't working.

I bought Tiny a small car so he wouldn't have to ask people to take him to his job. I wanted him to feel independent and free of worry about beggin' people to take him to work. Tiny and a lot of other people back home have a hard time keeping a job because they don't have cars and it makes it hard to be reliable about getting to work. But Tiny has the music hunger and so he won't get a job unless it is music related. Tiny is stubborn. You remember him, brushing his hair on stage when we were younger. That is the same man who won't get a job because he believes that he has got to concentrate on his music to make it happen someday.

That makes me look at this hunger for music that we all have. I think the hunger comes from a need to feel like we are succeedin' at somethin'. With limited education and limited resources, music is the only thing that makes us feel like we're a part of the world. It makes us feel worthy, because it comes to us so naturally. Music is *our* gift to the world. It's what we do. That's why I didn't push Tiny much because his hunger for music is the same as mine. The only difference is that I got a shot before him and he hasn't gotten his shot—*yet*.

The truth is that I love my family more than anything in my life. But when I come home to North Carolina, there is sometimes a pressure I feel of having to make everyone happy.

Helping the people who I grew up with in High Point is very important to me. If a few small moments in my life had gone differently, I could still be there in High Point, sitting next to my family on the couch and watching some other girl win *American Idol*. But handing out money on the streets is not really a way to help anyone. I can only help those who want to help themselves. That is why I reached back and took my brother Rico and my homegirl Aseelah on the road with me as background singers. The experiences on the road with me are career-makin' experiences that will take them into their own music careers. They are gaining experience performing and getting exposure to how the music business works. Because they have traveled the world with a signed artist, they will always get work with other signed artists. I wish I could do something that *real* for everyone.

I have a lot of dreams that I want for myself and my family. I want the people in my family know how much I love them and how I remember those nights on Montlieu Avenue, when we didn't have anything but the music. I keep working and doing shows so that we can have all the things that we deserve. I'm just hoping that soon the other hungers for those material things will wear off and we will soon be in plannin' mode and not *wantin'* mode.

I'm saving money, but I haven't invested yet other than buying a house. For now, I just want to save as much as I can, take care of my family, and learn more about how to manage money. One thing I know for sure is we are not going to look back. We're not going back to where we started.

One thing I do love is a bargain. I still shop at Target and Wal-Mart. If I could say anything to you, I would say be wise about how you spend your money. Don't buy designer clothes and fancy cars that you can't afford. Look for sales and look for bargains. If I could be at home more, you better believe that 'Tasia would be at yard sales. If I see a yard sale while on the road, I still stop if we have time. Going to yard sales reminds me that I am still a country girl and I don't have to splurge and spend a lot of money to feel like I got something.

I'm inspired by the bling-bling celebrities who have moved beyond the initial attraction of the bling and are now creating enough money to live comfortably without wasting money. I am inspired by Oprah Winfrey, who turned her broadcasting career into a television and publishing empire in addition to being an award-winning actress who always gives plenty of money to help other people. Now, that's what I'm talkin' about! Halle Berry does great movies, acts, and is a major model and film producer. Jay-Z, Puff Daddy, and Will Smith are smart men who turned hip-hop into fashion, restaurants, sports ownership, sneaker design, endorsements, and TV production. Someday, I want 'Tasia to be on that list.

Of course, I worry that I don't have the smarts to do things in business like they did even though it's what I want so much. All of these people at least finished high school, and I haven't even got my GED. I pray and ask God to give me the time and patience to finish my education, and the guidance to spend my money wisely, so there is always money in the bank. I have dreams of starting businesses. I want to open up a beauty shop that also has nail services. I have always wanted a restaurant and a club with live music, a small dance floor, and an open-mic night where musicians and poets can do their "thang." Sometimes, I even dream of a shoe store, because I love shoes so much. I would specialize in exotic European shoes. I also want to pay off my grandmother's church mortgage, which would be another family asset. And, because my grandmother has a daycare center in her home, I would love to expand it. All of my businesses would make jobs for my friends and the other people in High Point, who say there is no work available.

I have a lot of dreams. I must sound silly to you, but three years ago if I had told you I would be writing a book, I had traveled the world, and was the 2004 American Idol you and I would both have said that I was crazy. Having dreams are the first part of making things happen. Dreaming big means that you can think you can. If you are not dreamin' big, then you are just sleepin' on life.

MY MOMENT OF FAITH: WHAT I LEARNED

The rich ruleth over the poor, and the borrower is servant to the lender.

PROVERBS 22:7

- It is the small things that matter most.
- The best things in life are free.
- Rich people can be unhappy, and poor people can be happy. Money ain't everything!

9. Don't

Be a Hootchie

Mama

What is a hootchie mama? I'm sure you're wonderin'. And even though the term originated in the ghetto, it's a term that can be used all over the world for women who use their bodies to get what they want from men. This is a world problem; it's not a ghetto problem. It's sad to say, but women are trained to use their bodies and their looks to get attention and love from men. It's much easier for women who have no education or financial support to fall into this kind of thinking. The truth is, this is not a good place to be. And the reason that it's not a good place to be is because being totally at the mercy of a man and dependent on him takes away any belief that you have in yourself. You start to believe that you can't make it on your own. I felt like I had to be like that with J.B. until I went to *American Idol*. Even though J.B. was a good man and he was good to me, I don't want any of my sistas to ever have to feel like they can't do it on their own.

I have been fortunate to travel around the world, and although I don't know much about the cultures of other places, I do know that women everywhere want the attention of a man and they show it by the way they dress. In the ghetto where I come from, big butts and tight jeans are the way to get (certain) men's hearts, but the need for love is something that has no specific neighborhood or language.

You may be wondering why I would even put this chapter in my book. Who cares about hootchie mamas anyway? I care. And this chapter—and this book—is for everyone who thought they had me and other hootchie mamas figured out because they thought they knew about us from the media. But they don't know our hearts. I want everyone, especially young people, to know that every human being is not necessarily what they look like. I named this chapter this way to get your attention. This chapter is not about hootchie mamas, really; this chapter is really about how they came to be and who they are on the inside.

The name "hootchie mama" comes from TV. Hip-hop and R&B videos always have the girls who don't have on enough clothes, shakin' their butts and hanging all over a man who has three other woman hanging on him too. In the videos, it seems that none of the women are upset about the other women hanging on the man. This image is what makes a hootchie mama think it's OK to share their man. It isn't.

Hootchie mamas are women who are wearin' too few clothes and too much jewelry. Hootchie mamas were put into those music videos to make the men in the video feel like they are desirable. Hootchie mamas ain't real. They ain't real people, they're just an image that has been taken too far. Hootchie mamas come in all colors, shapes, and sizes. When I'm on the road, I see lots of young girls wearin' tight stuff and showin' too much skin. Their boyfriends seem to like it, but I'm sure their fathers and mothers don't. I have heard little girls tell me that they had to sneak out to go to my concert and that their mothers would die if they saw what they were wearing. I used to think to myself, I'm not happy with what you're wearing either, but it's not my place to say anything. Except for in the pages of my book!

I don't even like the term "hootchie mama" because a lot of people using that term could be called the same thing. It's a term that's based on the way someone looks—how they are dressed—but I know a lot of hootchie mamas and I know what is in their hearts. Most importantly, I know myself and I ain't no hootchie mama—but some people would have called me that back in the day. The hootchie mamas I know are kind and generous. They are funny and optimistic. They are concerned about their kids as much as anyone else is. They just think that they don't have any other way of gettin' attention and making things better for themselves. Hootchie mamas wish that their children could become doctors and lawyers, just like every other mother wishes for her child. A hootchie mama's problem is that she probably doesn't know any doctors or lawyers, and if she does, it's usually not in a social way. The doctors she knows may be the ones who told her that she was pregnant for the first, second, or third time. The lawyers she knows may be the ones who defended her baby daddy. These lawyers are the ones who break the news that her baby daddy is going to prison because of what he did last year.

The hootchie mamas that I know from back home are proud, despite what they look like to everybody else. Despite that they have always lived in the projects, and always got welfare and can't get off it because they have no education, it seems smarter to not work and keep havin' babies, then going to get a minimum-wage job. The cost of day care is more than a minimum-wage job earns. These women stand tall and proud and most of them have found some level of self-esteem despite their circumstances. They believe that they are as good as anyone else. Very few hootchie mamas realize that they are not just like everybody else, or maybe they are. I think the truth of being a hootchie mama is not even the way that you dress or how much skin you are showing. I think being a hootchie mama is an attitude. It is a way of thinking about men and how much we think we need them to feel good about ourselves.

My days of being a hootchie mama started probably in the eighth or ninth grade. Those are the days that I was friskin' around and trying to get the attention of other guys, but mostly B. From me watching those music videos, I could see what all girls at that age see—to get a man you have to be sexy and being sexy meant taking off your clothes, or wearing as few clothes a as possible. I was fourteen and watching those videos instead of listening to my mama. I was seeing those handsome, well-dressed, cool men on the TV and wishing that they were real. I was wishing that they lived in High Point, so I could see them and experience them. I was feelin' frisky and wished for them or anyone who looked like them. Every teenage girl has the same problem. The magazines and the TV shows are always promoting sex—even down to the commercials. When you see a commercial for acne cream, they show the girl with acne and they show that she is home alone and doesn't have a date. Then they show that the acne cream has taken all the acne away and then the next couple of seconds the girl has dates and a bunch of cute guys around her. What message is this sending—that you have be attractive and perfect to get dates and to get men to pay attention to you?

The term "hootchie mama" started in the ghetto with R&B and hip-hop music, but it is a mainstream idea. It is the physical presentation of women and our deep need for attention from men.

When I was fourteen years old, I started being more daring with my clothes. I was buying my tops a little tighter and wearing my skirts a little shorter. When I would buy jeans, I would buy jeans one or two sizes too small. I remember being in the store with my friends and overhearing all kinds of conversations with mothers and daughters about how tight the jeans were and I could hear the mothers saying you can't wear those, they are too tight. The girls were desperate to get those tight jeans so they could wear them to school. What is so funny to me is that you never hear a conversation like that in a store for men. Men for some reason are not trying so hard to get our attention. Why is that?

Because I was always shoppin' with my friends when I would get a few extra dollars from singin', I didn't have those disputes. Because I spent so much time away from home, my mother was always shocked when she saw me, but there was nothing that she could say. Those too-tight jeans would hug my butt and make it look so much bigger than it was. Remember that song by Sir Mix-A-Lot, "Baby Got Back"? Well, that is how girls like us started cravin' a bigger butt. That song, which was a top-selling song, is how I learned what to wear to make my butt look bigger than it was. And I'm sure that I'm not the only one who got some tips about what to do to get their men.

I knew I was successful when I started getting looks from men when I walked past those guys who hang out at the corner gas station or those guys driving through the projects. They were checkin' me out and that is what I wanted.

When I think back on it, I used to think I wanted attention, but what I really wanted was love and acceptance. I wanted to be loved by the boys because that's what those videos promised. I thought that if I looked like those girls, the men who I liked would like me too. What I really wanted was all the love that my boyfriend was not givin' to me. When you spend your whole day watchin' music videos, your world gets real small and all you can think about is get-tin' a man or losin' your man and everything in between that. That's the case for girls all over the world. Those videos are such a constant companion, and you can get really sucked into them. And that's what I see when I'm on the road. I see little girls with clothes that are too small, too tight, and too short. I see T-shirts that say things like "My boyfriend is away," which suggests that it is OK for her to be with some-one else in her boyfriend's absence. Young women seem to think this kind of attitude is good and gives them freedom, but what it really does is further bad relationships between men and women, and that is goin' on all over the world, not just in the ghetto.

Another reason that I became a hootchie mama when I was younger was that all of my friends looked like that. I was tired of not being accepted. Dressing like a hootchie mama made me feel included. I looked like the girls in the video and the ones down the street: *finally I felt like everyone else.* I'm sure that happens to a lot of young girls who don't quite know how to fit in. It's the girls who are getting attention from men that make the other girls want to be like them and *that* is why there are more hootchie mamas around than we can count!

When I was being a hootchie mama, I was goin' against the voice inside my head that kept telling me I was different from everyone else and didn't need to try to be like everyone else. It was God's voice telling me that, but at that age, I in-sisted on being the same as everyone else—no matter how bad I looked and no matter what God was tryin' to tell me. That is just part of being a teenager, y'all. You can't help yourself.

Just because I used to be a hootchie mama doesn't mean I couldn't change, and that doesn't mean that you can't change either. You can change your clothes, but more importantly, I hope you change your mind about boys and wantin' their attention so bad. I hope this chapter inspires hootchie mamas to think again about who they are. And I also hope that this makes a difference for those people who judge all the hootchie mamas that they see. There is more to us than those clothes. We are still people underneath the tight shirts and short skirts, and as I always say, *people are people.*

Unfortunately, there are not a lot of ways to speak on this topic, without it sounding like a lecture. But because I am 'Tasia and I have lived it, I think that I'm in a better position than most to speak about it. I know that once upon a time, I needed to hear every single word that I'm sayin' and there was no one who was in the same position that I am today—someone who had *truly* been there. I needed some straight talk without fakin' or holdin' anything back. I wanted to make my life better, and most importantly I wanted to know how to change, so I could love myself, finally. I wanted to have the love and respect that I deserved in a world that sometimes forgets that people who don't finish high school, go to college, or have important jobs are still *good people.*

I am an ex–hootchie mama, and I always will be, no

matter what happens with my music. And I will always speak up for the girls who are like I once was, because they can change too, if they really want to. I am hoping that you do.

One thing that you all need to understand is that a hootchie mama really thinks she looks good when she sees herself in the mirror. That's the first thing anybody who is judgin' needs to know. Most hootchie mamas want to live in the world they see on the television screen. Besides dressing like what they see in the videos, they think differently than most people outside the TV screen. When everyone else thinks that the hootchies have a big butt and should hide it, hootchie mamas think the exact opposite. They think the bigger the better and the more you can show a man, the more men you will get. It's as simple as that. When you think you're judging them, they are judging you for not being sexy enough. Being sexy and desirable is real important in this society, and it's even more so in the ghetto, because if you succeed in being sexy and desirable, people think it means that you will never be without a man.

It may have been boredom that caused me to get up so early in the morning and get all dressed up like a hootchie mama just to walk my baby through the projects lookin' for attention or just "somethin' to do." I didn't think that I was lookin' for a man, but when I think about what I was wearin', I know deep down that I was looking for a man. I was that girl walkin' the projects and hollerin' at every man hoping to get a little somethin' extra—an extra wink or a special touch or a promise that the guy probably couldn't even keep. I used to look for the guys with the nice cars and the nicknames that described who they were. Those guys with names like T-Money or Ace-Love or Grip were the guys with the reputations. People were talking about them. They were legends in the ghetto. That was the kind of man I was trying to get. And when I walked through these projects I wanted to stand out from all the other girls, so I would put a little rhythm in my motion when I knew the guys were watching me. I would slow down my pace a little. I would wink at them and make sure they saw my butt. And if I had gotten their attention, they would call me over or take the cell phone out of their ear or put their car in park. Putting their car in park was showing that I was worth stopping for. That would excite me.

The conversations with those guys were always the same.

"What's up?" I would say.

"Whatcha doin' you? You look good, baby," they would say. "When can I take you out?" they would then ask.

"Whenever you want," I would answer.

I knew if one of these invitations really turned into a date, I could just get one of my girls to stay with Zion. That's the silent code with single women all over the world: whenever a man wants to take you out, your girls will help you make arrangements to be able to go. These conversations would all end with "I'll call you, baby," and I would wink at them and know that they would never call me. Most of them didn't even have my phone number or they couldn't give a home number of their own. When they couldn't give their own home number, it was obvious that they lived with some woman. The thing about those kinds of guys is that they were always slightly distant. Most of them sold drugs, and the others sold stolen electronics. They called it "stuff that fell off the back of a truck." Because they were involved in these "businesses" they didn't like a lot of people knowing where they were or where they lived. They usually lived with different girlfriends so they were not easily found. They talked to a lot of different girls, so they would have a group of girls to choose from if they needed to leave their current girlfriend's home and get a new one quickly.

Those conversations usually never amounted to much. But they were something I had to do. These conversations were "something to do." At the end of the day, my girls and I would compare notes and see how many of us had the same conversations with T-Money, Ace, or Grip. Usually, by the end of the day, we had all been promised a call. Those guys would never call, but we walked the next day, looking slightly sexier than the day before, hoping that someone really would call. Or that someone really would ask for our number. Or that someone really would call the number that we gave them. We just kept tryin', believin' that some day we would meet someone who would spend some time and get to know us. We hadn't considered what we were wearing might be why we just kept having those conversations and gettin' no calls. Isn't that how it is with women—we just keep hopin'.

I was settling for all kinds of bad imitations of men. The truth is that most of those guys were the same. They were the sons of unmarried mothers and none of them had daddies. The fathers in their lives had been high or drunk or "uncles" who were not their fathers but the boyfriend of their young mothers. These men that I was choosing from didn't know how to treat a woman except for what they had seen in the videos. They wanted us if we looked good and they didn't have to get to know us. They never make videos about getting to know someone. I'm telling you about those times because what I learned from them is simple: The way you dress determines the kind of man you are going to attract. You never really "get" a man looking like that because he is not looking to be gotten. Guys like that are not really looking for a woman. They are lookin' for hootchie mamas. Remember, hootchie mamas are not real. They are just video stars.

If you are an outrageous hootchie mama, if you go out with your body parts hangin' out, just know you are leaving nothin' to the imagination of a man. *Everything* you have is already out there. There is nothing to dream about or even to call about. If you have enough clothes on, then a man has the chance to see the other parts of you: your inner beauty and your personality. If a man isn't attracted to you because of those things, you probably shouldn't want him. The problem with being a hootchie mama is that you're creating relationships that are based only on your physical appearance. When you gain a few extra pounds or don't wear a short skirt one day, your man will be able to say, "You don't look the way you used to," and then he will eventually leave you to find someone who looks like you used to, because he wanted only one thing—a hootchie mama—which is what you were when you met him.

If a guy chooses you for something inside of you, he wants to be with you long enough to keep finding out who you really are. He cares about your personal characteristics, things like your smile, your sense of humor, the things that you dream about, the things that you want for your life, your children, your family—the things that *matter*. Instead, if you're behaving and looking like a hootchie mama, he's just thinking about how to take the rest of your clothes off.

I can't say that I don't understand this. I understand because I used to dress like that. Although I had so much more to offer, I wasn't sure it was enough to get a guy. I had my sweet spirit, my open heart, my generosity, my love of music, my vocal gift, and my special relationship with God. But I still thought I needed to dress sexy to get attention. The attention I was getting was crap. It was a whole bunch of bulls**t. Excuse me for my language, but it just makes me mad that I wasted so much of my time when I was younger trying to find a relationship, and I was goin' about it all wrong. No one told me—or maybe they did and I didn't listen (again!).

I remember the exact day that I wanted to stop being a hootchie mama. I was visiting a church with my grandmother and she asked me to please dress right. She said, "I don't want to see you in those crazy clothes you wear!" Although I knew what she was referring to, I didn't want to think of myself in those "boring" clothes that my grandmother had asked me to wear. Because my grandmother is a minister, she forgave me for a lot of stuff, but she would never tolerate my wearing hootchie clothes and "being nakit" as she called it. When we walked into the church we were visiting, I noticed several men lookin' at me. They were lookin' at me in a way that I didn't know how to handle. They didn't have gold teeth or cell phones. They were proper gentlemen. They were church-going men. One of them came over to me and asked if he could help me in the door by carrying my bag. My grandmother seemed used to it. I had never seen a man act like that in my life. I was in shock and I didn't know how to handle it. I just said yes quietly, not even knowing what I was agreeing to. When we sat down on the front row with all the other ministers and their families, I just sat there realizing that although the man was lookin' at me, he was lookin' at me in a way that I had never experienced. It made me feel better than all those useless conversations put together. I sat in that prayer service and promised God that I would put my clothes back on.

It was hard going back into the life that I had created with all of my girls and our hootchie uniform. They were lookin' at me like I was crazy when I suggested wearing a longer skirt. They just kept sayin', "You are not going to get any play," and that scared me into thinking the way that I used to: "What was I without the attention of men?" I knew this fear well because I had seen my aunts go through the same thing. But when we were with my grandmother we all were forced to cover up, and it was remarkable how popular we became when we went to visit other churches with my grandmother. I loved the feeling of those Christian eyes on me, but those men were out of my league. They were older than me and I didn't know how to be any other way than a hootchie mama.

Truth is, the way you dress and the way you carry yourself attracts a certain kind of man. Every woman wants good and loving attention from her man and wants to be able to say that she has a man who really cares about her. That is what I always really wanted—and still do today. In my early life, I didn't have any good examples of the kind of man that I now want and I couldn't admit that what I really wanted was love. I grew up seeing women and men fighting with each other, calling the police on each other, and cheating on each other. I saw them hitting each other a lot too. I thought that anger, lies, and violence were a part of what made a grown-folks relationship. That's all I ever saw.

Every human being wants to be loved for who they are, not what they look like. This is especially true for women. We want to be loved inside and out for our conversation, our smile, our spirit. There are so many more things that make a man fall in love with a woman. Being half naked and showin' all you got is *not* the way, even though it seems like the best way to get a man. It's the media that has set us up to think like this.

The first time a guy addressed me with "What's up, ho?"

I knew that I had to change *everything*. And I remembered that man at the church who offered to carry my bag, even though it wasn't even heavy. He just wanted to do it to make it easier for me. Suddenly I had new view of men. "Hey, ho" is a common greeting for the girls in the neighborhood. That's what we say to each other! Although we think it's a cool way of saying "What's up?" it really isn't cool and our children shouldn't hear us talk to each other like that and they definitely shouldn't hear our men talk to us like that.

If you have a child, like I do, you don't want your son or daughter to see you like that and hear you being disrespectful to anyone or disrespected by anyone, even your friends. Frankly, you have to keep your children away from all of that. You have to class up your life, especially if you have a daughter. Classing up your life means raisin' your standards. Being stricter about what you will or won't do. Knowing the things that you will or won't tolerate around you and your kids. Knowing what you will or won't say. That's showing class—having standards. Your daughter needs to know that she doesn't have to show her body to get attention. You have to be the good example. Let your children see you leaving something to a man's imagination—not only for your children's sake, but for your own sake, as well. Your man (or potential man) will wonder what you must look like under your clothes.

Mystery is what makes a man call, because he really is interested in finding out *more* about you. He may even think that you could be his wife, someday. A man doesn't really want someone who carries herself like a hootchie mama. Besides hootchie mamas are not the kind of woman he would want to introduce to his own mama. You can be a little sexy, but class it up, *please.*

I'm not here to give fashion advice, because every woman has her own unique style. For me, I try to wear pantsuits, because they can show some of my body—but not too much of it. I wear fitted shirts that show my femininity, but not too much of my skin. I wear stylish cuts and colors to show that I'm in music, and, of course, I wear some outrageous shoes to show that I still love to have fun and am a little rebellious. Being fully dressed can say as much about you or more than taking all your clothes off.

All I am asking of you, my sistas, is to take yourself more seriously. Set a good example for your children and their friends. It doesn't matter how high your heels are or even if you wear short skirts from time to time. What it mostly boils down to is how you carry yourself. Look like a woman who loves and respects herself, not like a woman desperate for a man's attention.

This chapter is dedicated to my sistas—all the women in the world. I write this chapter for all the women and the daughters who have felt that they don't have the love in life that they want. Good love in your life doesn't have to come in the form of a man. The best love in your life is your self-love.

MY MOMENT OF
FAITH: WHAT I LEARNED

For all flesh is as grass, and all the glory of man as the flower of grass. The grass withereth, and the flower thereof falleth away.

1 PETER 1:24

These are things to tell yourself:

- I am worthy of true love.
- I can truly make a man happy in other ways besides sex.
- I am somebody's mother, and my children need to be proud to tell other people, "That is my mama."
- I am proud of myself and I want to look like it.
- Lastly, tell yourself: I am going to shed those hootchie mama clothes to be the woman that I am becoming today.

10. Keep It Real

I have some things that I need to get off my chest. Writing this book has been a powerful and emotional experience for me because it freed me to remember the things that have been too painful for me to remember clearly or even talk about. Everything in this book has made me who I am, so at this point, I am feelin' all kinds of things. I am feelin' proud, accomplished, and afraid of what will happen to me now that I have kept it real. And I feel ashamed about many of the things that I have done. Being in the public eye is a hard place to keep it real. Most people have a hard enough time just keepin' it real within their own home with family and friends. Keepin' it real for the whole world to see is scary. But as my grandma says, "The truth shall set you free." I am ready to be free.

Some of these memories have been difficult to deal with, but I feel like I am a better person for sharing them with the world and getting all of my secrets out once and for all.

But while I've shared everything that I've been through, there are still a few things I need to say or I would not be totally real in tellin' my story.

Why is it so hard for people to keep it real? I don't know about yours, but my life has been filled with secrets. My personal secrets and my family secrets have come to haunt me throughout the years. Growin' up, I remember there were so many unanswered questions and mysteries in our house. Why is Rico's last name Washington and not Barrino? Why do my parents sleep in separate bedrooms? What was behind what happened to Aunt Rayda? Why did I need to hide the fact that I can't read very well? Why did Zion's daddy abandon her? Why did my father cheat on my mother? Why did my grandpa Neil beat my grandma? Seeking the answers to these questions has been difficult. No one ever wanted to talk about these things. But the unanswered questions have inspired me to look for truth in everything I do. That is one of the reasons for this book. Many of the answers to those questions have been found, and some require a little more exploration, but what remains the truth of these secrets is that beneath all of them, there lies a sticky mess called *shame*.

Take it from me, shame is a terrible thing to live with. It's the thing that keeps our heads down. It's the reason our baby daddies leave us. It's the reason my drunken grandfather hit his wife. Shame is the reason I couldn't read. It's my own shame and that of others who were too scared to say it out loud. It's my shame of not saying, "I'm having a difficult time reading." It's my teachers's shame in not admitting that their student couldn't read. It's the principal's shame in not wanting to admit that his teacher passed a student who couldn't read, and on and on and on. This shame is the reason that today I live with the secret of my illiteracy. But it is a secret no more. And my heart races just thinkin' about what this fact will mean to my future. The only other option would be to keep coverin' it up. Keep fakin' it. Keep makin' up excuses like "I didn't have time to look over the contract" or "I didn't know how to get there, so you should come get me" or "I left my license at home, you have to drive." I have had enough of keepin' secrets to hide my shame, and although it will be hard when all the secrets of my life come out, I will finally be free. I am ready.

When I first started getting into music, the phrase "keep it real" was all around me in the secular music that we all grew up listening to. It was in hip-hop songs referring to being real to the grittiness of your neighborhood and true to your race and true to the ghetto. In R&B it was about being true to someone who you loved. In jazz it was about being true to your instrument and not watering down the free-flow sound of "real" jazz. In rock, it was about keeping it loud and hard and strong. The realness of music took my heart. Music was the place other than church that I found peace.

My grandmother always taught us to be honest and truthful. She used to say you have to tell the truth even if you are right or wrong. That has stayed with me. And now, even though I have been wrong so many times in my life, I'm ready to keep it real with myself and the world. I hope that this inspires you to do the same thing in your own life. It's the only way to really live.

I have written a lot about High Point. I haven't said too many good things about it, but I'm tellin' the truth. High Point is my home, and I'm proud that my picture is the welcoming point for entering the city. I feel that it is OK that I say those things because *I was there.* A lot of young people in High Point are depressed. That is the truth. They wouldn't say it, if you asked them plain, but if you asked them to describe their lives they would admit they are doing nothin'. They have children, they have hopes for their children, but they don't even know how to begin livin'. High Point is a depressing place for anyone who is not a furniture-store owner. High Point is all about furniture and nothing else.

There are a lot of depressed people walking around High Point, and many of them feel like they will never get out. Some of them never will.

With the overall feeling of helplessness comes a big sense of laziness that I was once a part of. There were no jobs and no motivation to move forward and so I just laid around with my friends and family, waiting for the next thing to happen. You know, "somethin' to do."

When *American Idol* happened to me, it was as though

ice-cold water was thrown in my face and snapped me out of my haze. Suddenly, there were so many things to do, almost too many things to do and not enough time to do them. As the *American Idol* experience unfolded for me, it was important to me to take as much of home as I could carry. I was able to take my brother and my girl Aseelah on the road with me. I also tried to reach back by givin' my friend, J., a drummin' gig on my tour. J. only lasted a week. After he left the tour, I wondered whether he left because he was scared that he couldn't keep up with the Los Angeles musicians, who have a lot more experience than him. But the difference between those musicians and J. is that he had the gig, and those L.A. musicians didn't. When he left, I thought he really gave up on himself. I never gave up on him.

That made me mad and it really hurt me. When a door is opened for you, you have to step up your game. J. went home and no one told me until it was too late. I just hate that it went down like that, but being out here on the road carries a lot of pressure. There are so many things goin' on at once, and I didn't have enough time to try to convince him to stay. We had to replace the drummer fast. Music is a fast life, and if you truly hunger for music, like all great musicians do, the fastness is a necessary part of it. You have to dust yourself off and not let fear of messin' up slow you down. I know it all must have seemed overwhelming to J. I also know that the L.A. musicians were learning songs in only a few hours, and I think J. was scared that he couldn't do that. He could have done it, I know he could have, with our help.

Anyone with talent and hunger can succeed when given the chance. And even if you do mess up, let the boss fire you—don't fire yourself! Not when your dream is at stake. Don't miss out on opportunities, even if they seem scary. I wish I could call him today, but now there is probably bad blood between us. I would say to him, "Believe that you are as good as anyone else. Don't compare yourself to other people. You are your only competition, and you can do anything that you put your mind to!" I chose J. because I loved him and his drumming and I really wanted him to have an unbelievable chance for his future and a ticket out of High Point. He should have kept it real with me and I would have helped him get what he needed.

Who knows the real reason that J. left, without even telling me to my face? Maybe, like so many of my friends, he wasn't able to read music. If that's true, maybe that shame made him feel like he couldn't do it. That's just another dream that shame has squashed.

To keep it real hurts. It hurts to uncover so much secrecy and answer so many unanswered questions. To see so many of the people that I grew up with not reaching their dreams is hurtful. If I could do it, *anyone* can do it! It pains me to see the weight of High Point's boredom weighing everyone down. I'm sure that there are more towns like High Point tucked away in America where young people are givin' up on their dreams. If I could do something, I would say, "Help!" I would say that to all folks in the small cities and all the kids feelin' lost in the big cities in America. I would say that the young people in America need your help. If a young person is being passed through high school just because a teacher doesn't want to deal with him, those teachers don't realize that they are ruinin' a whole life. That decision will affect all the other lives that will touch this young person's life through the hurt and shame that comes with lack of education. The impact goes on and on and on.

It's time for everyone to keep it real. If you can't do something because you don't know how to do something, you have to speak up. There's no longer room for bein' ashamed or keepin' junk a secret. Like my album says, "Free yourself."

When I'm keepin' it real with my fans I have to first say thank you from the bottom of my heart. I love y'all. But I wouldn't be 'Tasia if I didn't keep it real with you, too. Those of you who have met me know that I'm always happy to take pictures with y'all, give hugs, sign autographs—anythin' you want. But the one thing that upsets me is when someone is rude and acts like I have to do these things. I appreciate so much that so many of you voted for me and helped me get my music out there. I love to sing my heart out and I made an album and did a tour so that you could see me in person and share my music with me. I also love going to the radio stations across the country to keep in close touch with my fans. I don't want to feel like I have to do these things. I want to do these things because I love y'all and I appreciate your love.

Also, y'all do know that I love to eat. I would like to ask

all my fans for one little favor. When I sit down in a restaurant, it's the only time on the road that I can enjoy a meal and take a little break. I'm always happy to talk to you and sign autographs and take pictures with you and your children—as soon as I'm finished eating and as long as time allows but I would really appreciate it if you would wait to show me your love until *after* I eat. Think of it as givin' me your love by letting me eat!

Lastly, as much as I love y'all, I can't come to all of your houses or call your mother on the phone from the mall. Please just treat me like your home girl and don't ask me to do things that are outrageous. You know, I hate saying no, but some of those things you ask me to do are impossible and I just can't do it!

To keep it real with my music, my music and my story reach people of all races and all ages. My music is R&B, but my singin' is inspired by the Holy Spirit, which is universal. I have sung at the Kennedy Center for Elton John. I have sung with Patti LaBelle, who invited me to sing with her (which rarely happens). I have been on every national talk show several times over. I have sung for Oprah Winfrey. My music is not just black music and that is *proven*. Look at me. The black audience alone didn't get me to over a million CDs sold. My music is not just a ghetto thing. It's not only people in the ghetto who go through hard times. It's not only people in the ghetto who are single parents. It's not only men in the ghetto who leave their families. Whether it's because of being broke and immature or because the corporate father is having an affair with his secretary, bad men and bad people exist everywhere. Sit down and watch Maury Povich, and you'll see all kinds of women who have been beaten and abandoned. *Everybody* is goin' through *somethin'*. I have songs that everybody can relate to.

Y'all know that I want to go as far as I can in the music business, and I believe the sky is the limit for me. I love all music. I know all music. I won't be stuck in the ghetto category. I'm just not havin' it. Look at the things I've done. *And let me show you what else I can do.*

To keep it real with Zion, I have to write about the hardest things that any mother thinks about. What do I say to Zion about my life, which has been pretty full of drama since the day I turned five and the Holy Spirit entered my life? How do I tell Zion that the Spirit was in me and I still fought it for years, staying out of school, getting pregnant so young, and not listening to my parents?

Zion, I want to tell you how much I love you and how proud I am that you are my daughter. I also want to tell you that I have learned a lot in the last few years and some day I will be able to share it all with you. For now, I want to apologize to you for not being in your life and leaving you with your grandmother so much. You are in good hands with her. She is my best friend and she is like a sister to me. She has helped me with everything in my life, including taking care of you. I hope that when you grow up, someday, you will be able to say the same thing about me. I want to be your mother, but I also want to be your friend. When you get to be a big girl, then, maybe we can talk about all the things that I have done and all the choices that I have made that have changed your life already, and you don't even realize it.

When you start school, you'll be asked who your mommy is and why she's never at home. People will ask you why your grandmother and grandfather don't speak to each other. They will ask you where your father is and why he doesn't live with you.

It's a long story and it will take years for me to make you understand. This book is the beginning of me telling you all about our lives—yours, mine, Grandma's and Great-grandma's.

We have all had it hard, Zion, and the reason I'm away so much is because I don't want you to have to say that you too had it hard. I've had it hard enough for the both of us, and I work so hard so that your life will be good. But the thing about life is that the things that I need to work out for myself are the things to make life better for you, at least what I think will make it better for you.

When I was growing up, Zion, I didn't have any of the things you have. I didn't have my own pretty pink room. I didn't have a canopy bed with a sheer curtain over it, just like a princess. I didn't have new shoes and new church outfits every Sunday. I didn't have a lot of toys, and the ones I had were not brand name and on TV. I didn't have the kind of toys that light up and make noises. I didn't have any of those things. It was a different time and place and very different time for my parents—your grandparents.

But all you need to know is that God looked after us. God gave me a special gift with my voice and with that gift, He made everything possible for us. Singin' is why I'm away so much. God has given me my dream, and in return, I have promised Him that I would bless your life with what He has given me.

I guess if I'm going to keep it real, Zion, I know that you want to know where your father is and why he has not been around. Both of us were really young when we met. Although it sounds silly to say now, I loved your father, or at least I thought I did. It's hard to admit it to you, but he didn't love me, which is why when he knew you were going to be born, he left us. Having a little daughter was too big of a thing for him to do and so he stopped comin' around. Zion, I think he stopped comin' around because he couldn't handle a love that big. He just couldn't handle it.

The last thing I have to tell you is about the music. Music has made our family who we are today. Ever since my mama was young I've been singing with that special gift that God gave me and your grandmother and grandfather and all of grandpa's brothers too. Music saved our life, Zion, and it will always be a part of it. You already love music now, and I can't wait for you to get older so you can listen to it with me and know what kind of meaning it has had for our whole family. I want you to remember that music is evidence of God on Earth. I will have many years to explain to you the things about our family that are hard to understand, but for now, the first lesson I have for you is always tell the truth.

Whether you are right or wrong, tell the truth so you will never walk in shame. That's why I'm telling you these things now. I don't want there to be any secrets between us. I promise you that.

Zion is the place that the disciples went to pray in the Bible. I chose that name for you so that you will always be reminded of what to do when life gets hard.

At the end of every long, hard, exciting day, I know my toughest job is to keep it real with myself. Even though I have made it this far, my life is not perfect. The story is still goin' on. I laugh, I cry, I hurt, and I have drama goin' on from time to time. Life is always going to be full of trials, but the trials keep me growin' and make me stronger. I still have a smile on my face. When I see how far I've come, after all I've been through, I am happy.

There is one thing that I wish I could change, but I can't, at least not yet. I am still a single working mom, and no matter how much help I have from my mother, I can't be there for my child like I want to be. Zion needs me. I'm sure that other single working mothers have the same problems. I'm always torn between giving it all up just to be with her every night and give her a bath and hear her learn a new word and working hard to provide the things that she needs to have a better chance than I ever had in my early life. All that I'm missing is painful. It's a sacrifice. It's probably the biggest sacrifice that I'll make in my life. But when this early part of her life is over and she gets a good education and has a safe and happy place to live, I'll feel good that I've provided that kind of life for her. She knows I love her. The hugs and the kisses that I want to give her, I send over the phone lines. It's the best I can do for now.

Like I've said, I regret a lot of the choices that I've made. And even my music success can't take all of the pain away from the mistakes I've made. I still need to get my GED so I can tell my daughter that I have a diploma. I still need to get a driver's license so I can drive my daughter to the places that she will need to go when she gets a little older. I still am not the perfect mother. I still struggle with being only twenty-one and being a mom. I hate to admit it, but there are times I would rather go shopping with my girlfriends instead of having to deal with Zion, the stroller, the car seat, and all of those things that make the simplest things a struggle. But at least I can provide for my child, and that is a big thing coming from where I come from. I will get better at this motherin' thing with time.

I'm a dreamer, and so sometimes I say things like, "If I could go overseas right now and build schools, I would." That's one of my dreams. Those are the things that I want to do: travel, help, and give. But when I'm being real with myself, I know that someday soon I will have to stop working so hard to help other people like my family and High Point friends and figure out how to help myself more and prepare for my future and for Zion's future. I have a lot of responsibility, and when I'm being real with myself it's hard to deal with sometimes. I feel like I'm behind the starting line. I'm behind before I even begin.

I always write in a little notebook that I keep with me, "When you give it shall be given back to you. When you bless others, you are blessed." I have done that, many, many times over. Now, it's time to truly bless myself.

I'm out of things to tell you about my life and I don't know about your life. I'm just a young girl from a rough background who has had some success. I shared my life with you in the hope that if you see something, like a mistake you're making in your own life, maybe my story can help you make a change before it's too late. All I can say to you is the way to be real with other people is being real with yourself. Know that you are a child of God and treat everyone with the same respect that you want, because they are children of God too. Every relationship you have with another person should be sacred. Your relationship with your mother, brother, friend, boyfriend, or girlfriend should make you feel good. If it doesn't make you feel better about yourself, it's not a good relationship for you. Love and honor your children and your parents. But most of all, promise 'Tasia that you will forgive yourself for whatever you have done, and love every bit of yourself.

MY MOMENT OF
FAITH: WHAT I LEARNED

This is the scripture that I think about every single day before I put my feet on the ground. It gives me strength and peace. It will do the same for you too—just read it. God bless you.

In thee, O Lord, do I put my trust; let me never be ashamed: deliver me in thy righteousness.

Bow down thine ear to me; deliver me speedily: be thou my strong rock, for an house of defence to save me.

For thou art my rock and my fortress; therefore for thy name's sake lead me, and guide me.

Pull me out of the net that they have laid privily for me: for thou art my strength.

Into thine hand I commit my spirit: thou hast redeemed me, O Lord God of truth.

I have hated them that regard lying vanities: but I trust in the Lord.

I will be glad and rejoice in thy mercy: for thou hast considered my trouble; thou hast known my soul in adversities;

And hast not shut me up into the hand of the enemy: thou hast set my feet in a large room.

Have mercy upon me, O Lord, for I am in trouble: mine eye is consumed with grief, yea, my soul and my belly.

For my life is spent with grief, and my years with sighing: my strength faileth because of mine iniquity, and my bones are consumed.

I was a reproach among all mine enemies, but especially among my neighbours, and a fear to mine acquaintance: they that did see me without fled from me.

I am forgotten as a dead man out of mind: I am like a broken vessel.

For I have heard the slander of many: fear was on every side: while they took counsel together against me, they devised to take away my life.

But I trusted in thee, O Lord: I said, Thou art my God.

My times are in thy hand: deliver me from the hand of mine enemies, and from them that persecute me.

Make thy face to shine upon thy servant: save me for thy mercies' sake.

Let me not be ashamed, O Lord; for I have called upon thee: let the wicked be ashamed, and let them be silent in the grave.

Let the lying lips be put to silence; which speak grievous things proudly and contemptuously against the righteous.

Oh how great is thy goodness, which thou hast laid up for them that fear thee; which thou hast wrought for them that trust in thee before the sons of men!

Thou shalt hide them in the secret of thy presence from the pride of man: thou shalt keep them secretly in a pavilion from the strife of tongues.

Blessed be the Lord: for he hath shewed me his marvellous kindness in a strong city.

For I said in my haste, I am cut off from before thine eyes: nevertheless thou heardest the voice of my supplications when I cried unto thee.

O love the Lord, all ye his saints: for the Lord preserveth the faithful, and plentifully rewardeth the proud doer.

Be of good courage, and he shall strengthen your heart, all ye that hope in the Lord.

PSALMS 31: 1–24

ACKNOWLEDGMENTS

God, I thank You for everything You've done for me. Out of all those blessings You have bestowed, God, You keep blessing me. I didn't do everything right, or cross every "T," but, in spite of that all, You keep blessing me. I'm not ashamed to tell the world about it, God. You are the pilot of this plane and I am thankful to be able to ride it.

Now I want to thank my family and for all they have done for me. That is *the* Love. Zion, you are always on my mind, and you are the strength when Mama's tired. To my angel, Diane Barrino, you are my hero and I want to follow in your footsteps. To my father, Joseph Barrino, I love you for being hard on me because it made me the strong person I am today. To my brothers: Rico, Tiny, and Xavier. Being the only girl, it was tough foolin' with you boys, but I know your love has always got my back. Grandma Addie: you are my strong woman and I love you so much. You are my pastor. To all my busy nieces and nephews, Auntie loves you and prays for you every day.

To all my friends, and especially my church family, this book is a shout out because it is something we all went through. Jenny, I love you and you are always there for me, and J.B., what up. And to my special friend, # 80, thank you, baby.

My fans, who I like to call my family. Thank you for the love and support. I hope you see how my struggle made me a strong person and how keeping the faith can do the same for you. It's made me who I am today.

Erin, I love you, girl, for never giving up on me. To Ryan Webb and Maya Maraj for all your hard work and dedication to this project, thank you. A special thanks to Simon Fuller, Iain Pirie, Camilla Howarth, Emma Quigley, Zach Duane, Tom Ennis, and the rest of the 19 family. To Gary Greenberg, for standing by me and keeping an eye out. To everyone at CAA, thank you. Love you, Clive Davis, and everyone at J Records. Also, Michael Broussard and Jan Miller at Dupree/ Miller & Associates for your support.

To my editor, Nancy Hancock, thank you for making my story into a real book. Thank you to the team at Simon & Schuster, especially Sarah Peach, Marcia Burch, Chris Lloreda, and Shida Carr, for their tireless efforts. Finally, thanks to Kim Green, my collaborator, for her skill, encouragement, guidance, and for helping me to tell my story.